The Lord's Prayer

THE LORD'S PRAYER

by

Jan Milič Lochman

translated by

Geoffrey W. Bromiley

WILLIAM B. EERDMANS PUBLISHING COMPANY
GRAND RAPIDS, MICHIGAN

Copyright © 1990 by Wm. B. Eerdmans Publishing Co.
255 Jefferson Ave. S.E., Grand Rapids, Mich. 49503

Originally published as *Unser Vater*
© 1988 by Gütersloher Verlagshaus Gerd Mohn

Printed in the United States of America

Library of Congress Cataloging-in-Publication Data

Lochman, Jan Milič.
    [Unser Vater. English]
    The Lord's prayer / by Jan Milič Lochman; translated by Geoffrey W.
Bromiley.
        p.   cm.
    Translation of: Unser Vater.
    Includes bibliographical references.
    ISBN 0-8028-0440-3
    1. Lord's prayer—Criticism, interpretation, etc.   I. Title.
BV230.L53   1990
226.9'606—dc20
                                          90-32756
                                            CIP

Contents

CONTENTS

Preface

Two prior decisions in my work as a teacher led me to consider our views of life in the light of the Lord's Prayer. A few years ago I wrote an outline of ethics from the standpoint of the Decalog *(Signposts to Freedom: The Ten Commandments and Christian Ethics)*. Shortly afterward I wrote an outline of dogmatics based on the Creed *(The Faith We Confess: An Ecumenical Dogmatics)*. I thus put myself under a certain constraint. Having expounded the two basic texts of ethics and dogmatics, could I fail to expound the third text, the Lord's Prayer? The classical Reformation catechisms had expounded all three, and in most of them interpretations of the three play a decisive role. Concentrating on the one thing necessary in faith and thought, they constantly singled out the three familiar and basic texts.

That normative thinker of the Czech Reformation, Jan Amos Comenius (1592-1670), made this point most impressively. Just before his death, in a moving little work entitled *Unum necessarium,* he inquired into the center of his life and work and finally summed it up as follows: "If anyone asks about my theology, then like the dying Thomas Aquinas (and I will shortly die), I will take a Bible and with my lips and in my heart I will say: 'I believe what is written in this book.' And if someone asks about my confession of faith, I will name the Apostles' Creed, for none is so short, so simple, so pithy, none brings the decisive things so excellently together, and none cuts so briefly across all controversies and points of conflict. If anyone asks about my formula of prayer, I will name the Lord's Prayer, for the prayer of the only-begotten Son, who came forth from the Father, is the best key to open the heart of the Father. If anyone asks about the standard by which I live, the answer lies in the Ten Commandments, for what is pleasing to God no one can tell us better than God himself" (*Unum necessarium* X, 9).

I agree with this statement of Comenius. It is still relevant today, and perhaps especially today. We live at a time when the Judeo-Christian consciousness has been perceptibly shaken. Elementary biblical knowledge is dwindling. This loss of substance is deplored not merely in the churches, which it attacks at the root, but even among many contemporaries who have the fate of Western culture at heart. I have heard many colleagues on other faculties ask how it is possible to understand, for example, the history of medieval art, if students have almost no knowledge of biblical motifs and their interconnections. Theology today has to face this situation. It must be provoked by it, not to mere lamentation, but to an attempt to present the substance of the Christian legacy in modern terms and to respond to the challenges of the day, not ec-centrically from an arbitrary margin, but from the true center.

We undoubtedly have this center in the three classical texts. Apart from their material contents, they point the way even formally. In their impressive brevity they are still relatively present to our consciousness in both church and culture. In their basic character they are clearly oriented to the future. They do not in any sense rivet our attention to the past. They are incomparably ecumenical, a treasure obviously common to all Christians and not limited to an exclusive denominational group or cultural province. These are traits which in my view ought to characterize all our theological work.

One might say all these things already about the Ten Commandments and the Creed. (My personal experience confirms it; it has encouraged me that my two books have come out in several languages, Asian as well as European, and have aroused interest in both Protestant and Roman Catholic circles.) But they apply especially to the Lord's Prayer. If there is a single text which binds all ecumenical Christianity together, and which is recalled not merely occasionally but unanimously in almost all services in all churches, it is the Lord's Prayer. Hence it is not merely by outward but by inward necessity that in the present book I close my studies of the basic texts of Christianity with an exposition and application of the Lord's Prayer.

Basel, June 12, 1987   Jan Milič Lochman

Note: In the German text the author explains that he chooses the title *Unservater* rather than the more familiar *Vaterunser* because the former is the customary usage among Protestants in his second home, Switzerland. He asks for understanding from readers who are accustomed to the more usual form.

Introduction

Praying and Drumming

Those who undertake to develop Christian perspectives relative to the Lord's Prayer run up against particular difficulties. The Ten Commandments and the Creeds are formulated doctrinal texts with an ethical or dogmatic orientation. The "Our Father," however, belongs obviously to the category of prayer. Hence the difficulty: Prayer is a movement of the heart, whereas theology is a conceptual exercise, a scientific effort open to objective testing and publicly presented. Can we combine the two? Might not the attempt at combination merely result in alienating them?

I believe that it is possible and even necessary to relate the two. The specific feature of theological work, not simply in contrast to other scholarly pursuits but with a notable difference of accent, lies in its attempt to take both elements into account and to bring them into cooperation. Theology is the thinking side of faith. Here the two elements are combined, though admittedly not without tension. Heart and mind cannot be separated from one another. It was no accident that at the head of his first dogmatic lectures Barth put the prayer of Thomas Aquinas: "Merciful God, I pray thee to grant me, if it please thee, ardour to desire thee, diligence to seek thee, wisdom to know thee and skill to speak to the glory of thy name. Amen."[1]

An old maxim of theological work points in this direction: The law of praying is the law of believing; we might also add, the law of thinking and the law of living. It is the basic law, or, better, the basic movement of theological existence. The formula occurs in Augustine and in such great medieval theologians as Aquinas and others. It also occurs in the Reformers; Luther has it in many forms. It relates first to the church's liturgy as a determinative norm of faith. What takes place in worship is not something solemn but theologically unrewarding and irrelevant. The liturgy does not take place outside theological reflection even though it transcends the conceptual. Conversely, and with even broader implications, theology takes place in the context of liturgy. It is itself a liturgical matter, though it has also to discharge other functions, for example, the task of rational wrestling with the truth entrusted to it, and the task of communicating it on the Areopagus of the day. Linking dogmatic deliberations to a prayer text does not entail the leap into another genre. It is not an impermissible sidestep.

Yet in such an enterprise there is another difficulty, less basic but more urgent in view of contemporary intellectual and sociological changes. Prayer is undoubtedly one of the oldest and most constant phenomena in the history of human religion and culture. It is no wonder that the church father Tertullian, contemplating the varied but impressively universal presence of attitudes of prayer in all nations, made his famous remark about the witness of the soul that is by nature Christian. Even in our secularized age prayer has not completely disappeared or become homeless. In recent years even the unchurched have shown increased interest in spiritual exercises and meditation. Yet prayer in the precise sense, as direct and purposeful invocation of God, has become unintelligible and even unbelievable to many people today.

1. See E. Busch, *Karl Barth,* tr. John Bowden (Philadelphia: Westminster, 1976), pp. 154-55.

There are good reasons for this development that theologians must take seriously. Dorothee Sölle has drawn attention to one of the most important in her essay "Gebet."[2] For the modern post-Christian consciousness, she writes, prayer has become a substitute action. When the captain of a ship in distress says that the only thing to do is to pray, the cry goes up from the chaplain: "Are things that bad?" This witticism describes the situation accurately. God is brought in when the intelligence cannot do anything, or can no longer do anything. Prayer comes into action when our own strength fails. In place of the independent secular action at our disposal, action which is responsible for itself, prayer has a role in certain emergency situations, but only as an illusion, a flight, a substitute action when we are not capable of real action or not willing to engage in it.

A familiar incident in Brecht's *Mother Courage* illustrates how little credibility prayer has when it is viewed in this way. When the peasants were helpless against advancing soldiers, the dumb Kattrin was urged to pray. Nothing could be done to prevent the shedding of blood. The peasants were weak and had no weapons; they had nothing on which to rely. They were in God's hands; only he could help. But the dumb Kattrin, instead of praying, began to beat on a drum in order to awaken the inhabitants. She was shot down, but the city was ready to resist.

Dorothee Sölle comments that this extreme case brings to light an old misunderstanding of prayer, namely, that of substituting words to a higher being for acts on behalf of those around us. The drumming of Kattrin shows that devout and subjectively genuine prayer can be an excuse for those who will not become involved. If we ask Christians what they did for Jews during the persecution, the most mendacious answer is: "We prayed for them."[3]

2. D. Sölle, "Gebet," in *Theologie für Nichttheologen* (Stuttgart: 1966), pp. 102ff.

3. Ibid., p. 103.

In these deliberations Sölle is close to Dietrich Bonhoeffer. In his *Letters and Papers from Prison* Bonhoeffer writes very impressively about the way in which religious themes like God and prayer have been pushed into a corner in the course of contemporary secularization. They are little more than stopgaps (and prayer is a substitute action). To most thinking people they are beyond belief. A world come of age needs a religionless interpretation of the Christian cause. For Bonhoeffer this is the real challenge to modern theology. But for him (and for Sölle) this task does not mean giving up prayer. It means a more relevant and credible readoption of it, not in an unenlightened, generally religious, magical, or self-centered sense, but in the sense of the Bible and Jesus, as an act of the heart that is moved on behalf of justice. Bonhoeffer finds the basic structure of the Christian life in the prayer and action of the righteous. As he pithily puts it, "Only he who cries out for the Jews may sing Gregorian chants."[4]

But those who do cry out for the Jews, those for whom doing righteousness in a social context is important, *should* sing Gregorian chants. If prayer is highly suspect as a substitute action in evasion of responsibility, an activism without the perspective of prayer—an evasive busyness as a substitute action for the life of prayer—is a theological temptation, and one that perhaps today is no less real than the first. The example of Bonhoeffer himself helps us to avoid drawing too hasty a conclusion. The papers from prison include many poems and prayers that clearly focus on this concern of Christian existence. The witness of those around him bears out this impression. I will cite only that of the prison doctor in the last minutes before Bonhoeffer's execution. "Through the half-open door in one room in the huts I saw Pastor Bonhoeffer, before taking off his prison garb, kneeling on the floor praying fervently to his God. I was deeply moved by the way this lovable man prayed, so devout and so certain that God heard his prayer. . . . In the almost fifty

4. E. Bethge, *Dietrich Bonhoeffer: Man of Vision, Man of Courage,* tr. Eric Mosbacher, et al. (New York: Harper & Row, 1970), p. 512.

years that I worked as a doctor, I have hardly ever seen a man die so entirely submissive to the will of God."[5]

This example might help to elucidate the place of prayer in our post-Christian culture, or, better, our own situation as we engage in prayer today. There can be no doubt, says Sölle, that with a better understanding of the world the things in uncontrolled nature that drove us to prayer are far fewer. Quantitatively there are probably less individuals praying now than for hundreds of years. But this less can be more. For as the scope for the remaining magical elements and incantations has shrunk, enlightenment might help prayer to come to its true self.[6]

The Modes of Prayer

"Help prayer to come to its true self." But what is prayer according to the Bible? Let us attempt a short sketch.

Prayer is the response and vital side of faith. Believers pray; those who pray believe. "I believe, Lord; help thou mine unbelief" (Mark 9:24). This classical New Testament confession of faith is a prayer. It shows the place of prayer. Its context is our need or necessity before God. If we do not feel and recognize this need, and our need to be freed from it, prayer ceases or is perverted. It ceases if we think we can lay aside the question of God, the question concerning God, as an outdated and meaningless question of our own cultural history or the history of world culture. It is perverted when the devout or orthodox (the self-righteous) believe they can meet their need before God by merits or credits. When we think that our own verdict can bind God and his judgment, the praise of God becomes self-praise, pseudoprayer. We recall the story of the Pharisee and the publican (Luke 18:9-14). When we either cease to pray or pervert

5. Ibid., pp. 830-31.
6. Sölle, *Theologie für Nichttheologen*, p. 103.

prayer, the unrest of faith is stabilized, the tension of the question of God is released. Self-confirmation is found in either our "having" or our "not having."

Prayer is a protest against such self-confirmation. It is a step into the open, with no guarantee but also without resignation. It is part of the battle for God, like Jacob's wrestling at the Jabbok and saying "I will not let you go, unless you bless me" (Gen. 32:22ff.). Those who wrestle and pray biblically do not rely on their own virtues or the ardor of their practice of piety but on the promise that is given them. Luther expressed this when he said that he did not dare to pray to God because of his own devotion or holiness but because from the lips of God's Son there had come the promise that those who ask, receive. The heart might not be ardent or fervent enough, but Luther built upon the Word.[7]

In this sense biblical prayer is more than verbal prayer. The apostle speaks about praying without ceasing (1 Thess. 5:17). Clearly we have here a whole dimension of human existence before God. Prayer as this inner dimension embraces and accompanies the whole polyphony of human life. In this sense all thoughts and actions that respect God and his creation are acts of prayer. Prayer concerns what the Czech philosopher and statesman T. G. Masaryk continually described and lived out as life from the standpoint of eternity. Yet this understanding of our situation before God calls for concrete and specific expression, for prayer in the full sense of the word, for the articulated word of prayer. John Calvin bore impressive witness to this saving necessity of prayer, not as a duty, but as the liberating representation of God's all-embracing turning to us: "Surely, with good reason the Heavenly Father affirms that the only stronghold of safety is in calling upon his name. By so doing we invoke the presence both of his providence, through which he watches over us and guards our affairs, and of his power, through which he sustains us, weak as we are and well-

---

7. *D. Martin Luthers Werke: Kritische Gesamtausgabe* (Weimar, 1883ff.), 34/1:379-91.

nigh overcome, and of his goodness, through which he receives us, miserably burdened with sins, unto grace."[8]

From this comprehensive and many-faceted nature of prayer, the various forms result. Of the biblical fulness, following 1 Timothy 2:1, we might mention especially three: petition, intercession, and thanksgiving.

It is to the human situation of need before God (and in God's world) that petition especially and directly relates. In the New Testament the range of petitionary prayer is very broad; it deals with small things and great. The apostle could pray that his plans for a journey might work out (Rom. 1:10), but we also find the prayer that the terrors of the last day will not come in winter (Mark 13:18). There is confidence that the Father will see to our earthly welfare (Matt. 6:25ff.), but prayer also for the coming of Christ (1 Cor. 16:22; Rev. 22:20).[9] Life in all its diversity is brought before God in petition.

No sphere of human life, and especially no urgent human need, lies outside prayer's terms of reference. Even fear of a magical misunderstanding of prayer ought not to cause us to make the spiritualizing or existentializing mistake of thinking it intellectually unworthy or theologically unenlightened to pray for specific physical and secular needs. The apostle is rightly much less inhibited when he tells us that if any are sick, then let them pray (Jas. 5:13-15). We see at once that any physical or mental illnesses are in view. The word of faith and promise applies to the sphere of material life as well: "The prayer of a righteous man has great power in its effects" (5:16).

Along with petition stands intercession. The link between them is decisive for our understanding of New Testament prayer. In prayer human need is not isolated; the personal and the social go together. People pray for one another in the Chris-

8. Calvin, *Institutes of the Christian Religion*, 2 vols., tr. Ford Lewis Battles, ed. John T. McNeill (Philadelphia: Westminster, 1960), 2:851, § 3.20.2.
9. Cf. E. Lohse, "Gebet," in *Evangelisches Kirchenlexikon*, 4 vols., ed. Heinz Brunotte and Otto Weber, 2nd ed. (Göttingen: Vandenhoeck & Ruprecht, 1961), 1:1436.

tian community, but they also pray for the world. Intercession is a sign of concerned participation in the fate of others. Jesus constantly laid this task upon the hearts of the disciples, and the apostles laid it upon the hearts of the churches. Prayer breaks through the narrow private area and becomes part of our social and political service of God: "First of all, then, I urge that supplications, prayers, intercessions, and thanksgivings be made for all men, for kings and all who are in high positions, that we may lead a quiet and peaceable life, godly and respectful in every way" (1 Tim. 2:1-2).

A further development along this line is the third form of prayer, thanksgiving and worship. Very concretely we have prayer here too. Faith is receiving and enjoying life with all its great and little opportunities as a gift that is ever new. Thanksgiving stands opposed to the way in which we, satiated and bored, take the everyday for granted, so that life becomes dull. But thanksgiving goes beyond that. Paul emphatically and constantly gives thanks for brothers and sisters in the faith, for the churches, even though they might disappoint him in many ways. Above all and in spite of everything he found a final and unconditional cause for thanksgiving in faith and in experience of the liberating nearness of God, of salvation in Christ, of hope for himself and the world. Logically, then, as we see especially in the Psalms and in New Testament doxologies, the final thing in prayer is praise of God.

In these three forms we have an outline of the basic structure of prayer from a biblical and theological standpoint. Petition, intercession, and praise: The plurality safeguards us against any impoverishment of the life of prayer. There are also other modes—for example, complaint. It, too, is prayer. The Bible neither forbids it nor censures it. Indeed, a whole biblical book bears the title Lamentations. There are also express songs of complaint and accusation in the Psalms. On the margin, and very problematical from the New Testament standpoint, though humanly understandable in the last resort, there are even psalms of revenge. Overcoming this human temptation has a place before God. Finally, not on the margin but at the center of the

Bible, at the cross of Jesus Christ, there is the cry of dereliction: "My God, my God, why [to what end] hast thou forsaken me?" (Mark 15:34; cf. Ps. 22:1). Unquestionably this cry from the depths, this protest against failure, betrayal, abandonment, and suffering, is also part of the fulness and totality of human life before God.

In this regard one should note that Christian prayer is more than an instrument and expression of the pious (or, in secular terms, the meditative) self-understanding. It does relate to the self, to the inner life of faith: "It's me, O Lord, standing in the need of prayer." But it is also a matter of our understanding of God and the world, of the need of others, of the glory of God. We should not play off these elements against one another or reduce them to one another. To use Anselmian language, prayer is not a *monologion* but a *proslogion*. In the quiet room we are not shut in with ourselves when we pray. On the contrary, we are alongside others and in the presence of God. This is the truly liberating aspect of prayer. Prayer is a special opportunity—made special by the promise—not to lose ourselves in our own wandering thoughts and self-seeking desires and expectations, or if possible to bring them to fulfilment, but to be free of them.[10]

In this sense prayer can be the most faithful act of living for others. It can be the test and proof of the seriousness of our fidelity to them. The command of Jesus points the way. Without forgetting personal needs, even those that are material, it leads us out into the open field of the history of God, not alone, but all of us together. *Our* Father is the address.

Understood in this way, prayer is a center of renewal for the life of faith. The great emphasis of the biblical witnesses on this dimension shows its relevance. Without it faith would be no less dead than it would be witout works. It gives us space. Our need for prayer is our need for spiritual and mental breath. In it we reach beyond ourselves to that which saves, to a new beginning.

10. Cf. H. G. Ulrich, *Glaube und Lernen*, 1/1 (1986), p. 17.

Our Identity in Prayer

In prayer we reach beyond ourselves, not to lose ourselves but to find ourselves. A vital question arises here, that of our true identity as human beings and as Christians. It is an urgent question today. Who am I? In the net of conditions and relations, of manipulations and determinations, who am I truly? Here again I find Dietrich Bonhoeffer especially helpful. In his *Letters and Papers from Prison* we find among his many prayers and verses the poem "Who am I?" In it he looks at the rift between the outward image that he presents and the way in which he understands and experiences himself. He cannot reconcile the two. A crisis of identity? The last lines of the poem read:

> Who am I? This or the other?
> Am I one person today, and tomorrow another?
> Am I both at once? A hypocrite before others,
> and before myself a contemptibly woebegone weakling?
> Or is something within me still like a beaten army,
> Fleeing in disorder from victory already achieved?
>
> Who am I? They mock me, these lonely questions of mine.
> Whoever I am, thou knowest, O God, I am thine.[11]

The psalmists saw their lives like this. In the alternation of experiences, in the struggle for meaning and the orientation of existence, in contrasting situations and the clash of perspectives, they were who they were before God. From the standpoint of the story of Christ, the apostle formulates precisely the same truth: "Your life is hid with Christ in God. When Christ who is our life appears, then you also will appear with him in glory" (Col. 3:3-4). Because this is so, because the identity of our life is grounded in God and thus persists through every temptation, attack, and break, prayer is an appropriate element and instrument of life for those in search of meaning.

11. Dietrich Bonhoeffer, *Letters and Papers from Prison: The Enlarged Edition*, tr. Reginald H. Fuller, et al., ed. Eberhard Bethge (New York: Macmillan, 1972), p. 348.

In this insight and conviction Christians can follow the example and cling to the promise of Jesus. It is striking how important prayer was for Jesus, though he did not make a show of it. On the contrary, he sharply and emphatically attacked those who make prayer a spectacle—only hypocrites do that (Matt. 6:5ff.). Yet he laid all the more emphasis on prayer as quiet, intense communion with God. The Gospels tell us again and again that Jesus withdrew to pray (e.g., Mark 1:35 par.; Luke 5:16), and even that he spent the whole night in prayer (Luke 6:12). In critical hours especially he found in prayer new strength to withstand the assault of the tempter (Matt. 4:10 par.) or in severest temptation to win through to the will of the Father (Mark 14:36 par.). Even his last words from the cross, whether the cry of dereliction in Mark or "Father, into thy hands I commit my spirit" in Luke (23:46)—both quotations from the Psalms—are prayer.

Christians in prayer should have before them the promise as well as the precedent of Jesus. I have in mind the parting high priestly prayer in John 17, in which Jesus prays to the Father for his disciples, not merely for those present but also "for those who believe in me through their word" (v. 20). We may specifically think of the incident in Luke 22:31-32. For the self-confident Simon who will soon deny Jesus, the hour of satanic sifting and bitter failure has the promise of a new beginning, not in Peter's own power but in the faithfulness of his Master: "I have prayed for you that your faith may not fail." According to the New Testament this is the basis and hope of the Christian life. In spite of all our weakness we live and pray in the power of the prayer of Jesus.

It is in this light, in relation to Jesus, that we are to understand the direction and encouragement which transcends subjective helplessness and defeat and shows us the right way in the search for personal identity: "Ask, and it will be given you; seek, and you will find; knock, and it will be opened to you. For every one who asks receives, and he who seeks finds, and to him who knocks it will be opened" (Matt. 7:7-8).

11

The Prayer of Prayers

Phenomenologically, human prayer is uncommonly varied and many-faceted. Every possible flower and weed flourishes here. Often, especially in primitive times, prayer was simply a word of magic or power, an attempt to lay hold of powers or to enhance them. It was an appropriating of divine potencies, a cultic manipulation for one's own ends. Higher religions, and certainly biblical piety, have moved away from this magical understanding. But remnants remain as religious people are notoriously tempted to hitch God to their own wagons.

The theological question thus arises: What is the nature of responsible Christian prayer? In relation to our need of prayer the apostle points emphatically to the redemptive spontaneity of the Holy Spirit. He writes in Romans: "The Spirit helps us in our weakness; for we do not know how to pray as we ought, but the Spirit himself intercedes for us with sighs too deep for words" (8:26). Yet the comforting pleading of the Spirit in no way releases us from the task of asking what is appropriate in prayer. This question is raised and answered in the New Testament. It lies unmistakably in the background of the Lord's Prayer.

As is well known, we have two versions of this prayer in the Gospels. They are set in different contexts, but both answer the same question: How and what are the disciples to pray? This is especially clear in Luke. Here the disciples come to Jesus directly with the request: "Lord, teach us to pray" (11:1ff.). In so doing they refer to John the Baptist and his disciples, who had obviously received instruction in prayer from their teacher. Jesus' answer to the request is the Lord's Prayer. In Matthew the text of the Lord's Prayer lies at the heart of the admonitions of Jesus regarding the right way to give alms, to pray, and to fast. But here again we find an introduction that we can hardly misunderstand: "Pray then like this" (6:9ff.). In the mind of Jesus prayer is not a matter of preference or caprice. The spontaneity of prayer is oriented. The Lord's Prayer shows us the way of spiritual freedom.

12

What is the relation between the two versions? Let us look at the texts side by side.

Matthew 6:9-13	Luke 11:2-4
Our Father	Father,
who art in heaven,	
Hallowed be thy name.	Hallowed be thy name.
Thy kingdom come,	Thy kingdom come.
Thy will be done,	
On earth as it is in heaven.	
Give us this day our daily bread,	Give us each day our daily bread;
And forgive us our debts,	And forgive us our sins,
As we also have forgiven our debtors;	For we ourselves forgive every one who is indebted to us;
And lead us not into temptation,	And lead us not into temptation.
But deliver us from evil.	

Matthew has a longer text than Luke, for Luke does not have two petitions ("Thy will be done . . ." and "deliver us from evil") or the doxology, which is found in later manuscripts of Matthew. Luke also has the simpler invocation "Father." By the usual rules of textual criticism we regard the shorter text as older. The additions in Matthew seem to obey the general tendency of liturgical texts to value solemn structure. Yet some details point to the fact that even if it is later the text in Matthew preserves older motifs. Thus the word "debts" would seem to be more original that the later Greek word for "sins." In the petition for bread, too, Matthew seems to have an older text. The "this day" fits in better with the eschatological atmosphere of the prayer than the Lucan "each day."

On the basis of such considerations Joachim Jeremias has attempted the following reconstruction of the Lord's Prayer as Jesus originally gave it:

Dear Father,
Hallowed be thy name.
Thy kingdom come.
Our bread for tomorrow / give us today.
And forgive us our debts / as we also herewith forgive our
debtors.
And let us not succumb to temptation.[12]

This gives us the structure: (1) invocation; (2) two (or three) "Thou" petitions in parallelism; (3) two "We" petitions in parallelism; and (4) concluding petition (coupled in Matthew with one more). But other divisions are possible, and the early church soon proposed them with many variations. Thus in the Matthean version one might contrast and connect the first three and last four after the manner of the Decalog as relating first to God and then to human needs. Other expositors try to support this kind of division by material arguments, finding common Jewish thinking in the first part and special emphases of Jesus in the second. Yet one should not play off the two approaches against one another. As Ernst Lohmeyer rightly points out, "this dual standpoint must be true to a special degree of the prayer which is taught here. It is, in fact, 'only' a prayer, such as pious Jews of the time of Jesus would pray and teach, steeped in the words and thoughts of the Old Testament and suffused with its spirit, and it is equally and precisely in being this an eschatological *novum*, the way to the eternal life that the Master brings."[13]

The value that early Christianity set on the Lord's Prayer, emphatically so and without debate, was extraordinarily high. Though the apostolic Epistles have hardly any direct allusions to it, it obviously left its mark strongly in the primitive church. It did so at a central point, namely, in Christian worship. Thus the Didache quotes it in full, with the admonitory introduction

---

12. Joachim Jeremias, *The Prayers of Jesus*, Studies in Biblical Theology 2/6, tr. John Bowden, et al. (Naperville, IL: Allenson, 1967), pp. 94-95.
13. Ernst Lohmeyer, *"Our Father": An Introduction to the Lord's Prayer*, tr. John Bowden (New York: Harper & Row, 1965), p. 25.

to believers not to pray as the hypocrites but as the Lord commanded in the Gospel (8:2). They were to pray it three times a day, and the Didache already had the doxology: "For thine is the kingdom and the power and the glory."

Later testimonies give evidence of its prominent place in the liturgy, that is, at the eucharist. This means that the prayer was one of the spiritual treasures which were reserved for Christians as an especially precious part of their spiritual inheritance and which were not to be profaned. Even today we find something of this liturgical reverence in classical texts. In the East, in the Liturgy of Chrysostom, the priest says emphatically before it is prayed: "Make us worthy, O Lord, that we may joyfully and boldly venture to call upon thee, heavenly God, as Father, and to say: Our Father." The same is true at the Roman and Episcopalian eucharist: "We are bold to say [audemus dicere], Our Father."

Additional witness to the unique valuing of the Lord's Prayer may be found in the church fathers and Reformers. Sooner or later almost all of them undertook to expound it and made vital contributions to its theological understanding. I mention only Origen, Gregory of Nyssa, Maximus Confessor, Tertullian, Cyprian, Augustine, and all the standard Reformers from Hus to Luther and Calvin. Tertullian best brought out its theological significance when he pregnantly described it as a summary of the whole gospel. In this sense and, I hope, in this spirit, we will now turn to the individual clauses.

Our Father in Heaven

Look, What a Father

One cannot emphasize enough that the very first word of the Lord's Prayer is a decisive one that points the way. It is the word "Father." Whether we follow Luke and take it in all its simplicity, or Matthew with his liturgically expanded form ("Our Father, who art in heaven"), the first word is one that we cannot exchange: "Father." It sets the stage for our whole exposition of the individual petitions. In the history of exposition it has rightly been observed again and again that one's understanding of the whole prayer depends upon one's understanding of this first word.

This does not mean in the least that the meaning of the first word is self-evident. On the contrary, with all the associations that it evokes, and with the burden of its manifold use in the history of religion and culture, its specific meaning at the head of the Lord's Prayer may easily be misunderstood. Precision is needed.

To begin with, a brief grammatical note may not be superfluous. The word is in the vocative, not the nominative. It is address, invocation. In his detailed exposition of the first clauses of the Lord's Prayer (the final train of thought of his *Church Dogmatics*), Karl Barth has rightly and forcefully drawn attention to this fact. We do not have here something banal, but a basic rule for the legitimate use of the name of God. "Seriously, properly, and strictly Christians cannot speak *about* the Father but only *to* him."[1] Naturally, theology cannot avoid speaking *about* God as well. As we give an account of the faith, we have to use the nominative. But its use is valid only when we do not forget that it has to serve as a substitute for the vocative. This is why taking note of the form of speech in the Lord's Prayer is both methodologically necessary and existentially salutary in theological enterprises. In both life and thought only an attitude of address is appropriate to the reality of God. "Father as a vocative, whether expressed or not, is the primal form of the thinking, the primal sound of the speaking, and the primal act of the obedience demanded of Christians. . . . the primal form of the faithfulness with which they may correspond to his faithfulness."[2]

Materially, too, the use and content of the name "Father" needs to be made concrete and clarified. To call God "Father" has been common from an early time in the history of religion. In antiquity, for example, Homer calls Zeus "the father of men and gods." The reference is to their origin along the lines of divine generation and also to the overarching authority of the supreme god in the cosmic sphere. The great philosophers, too, made use of the concept, as when Plato in his *Timaeus,* in the context of the creation myth, called the idea of the good the father of all things. By way of Stoicism this description of God as Father became a common concept in Hellenistic religious philosophy and piety.

For the New Testament, the Old Testament background was much more important than that of religious history. In the Old Testament God was called "Father" only fourteen times, but many of these are very significant passages. His fatherhood was not linked to mythological motifs (divine generation) but to the events of salvation history. God showed himself to be a

---

1. Barth, *The Christian Life, Church Dogmatics,* IV/4: *Lecture Fragments,* tr. Geoffrey W. Bromiley (Grand Rapids: Eerdmans, 1981), p. 51.
2. Ibid.

Father to Israel by acts of saving power in history. This relation was especially decisive for the prophets. They bewailed the notorious ingratitude of the people: "A son honors his father, and a servant his master. If then I am a father, where is my honor? And if I am a master, where is my fear? says the Lord of hosts to you" (Mal. 1:6; cf. Deut. 32:6-7; Jer. 3:19-20). Recognizing its guilt, in spite of everything Israel can still appeal to the fatherhood of its God in the cry: "Thou art our Father" (Isa. 63:16; Jer. 3:4). And the divine answer shows clearly what this fatherhood implies in spite of the resistance of the people, namely, his unswerving pity: "Is Ephraim my dear son? Is he my darling child? For as often as I speak against him, I do remember him still" (Jer. 31:20); "Can a woman forget her sucking child, that she should have no compassion on the son of her womb? Even these may forget, yet I will not forget you" (Isa. 49:15). The latter saying, it is true, refers to a mother rather than a father, but it can be quoted in the present context. Apart from the central motif of God's infallible faithfulness, it is noteworthy because it repels the idea that there is sexism in the theme of God as Father. The biblical motif can find a place for maternal characteristics in its central intention.

The Old Testament concept of God as Father helps us to understand the invocation of the Lord's Prayer. But the decisive material content comes from the New Testament itself. For God's fatherhood plays an important role in the New Testament, both in the understanding of Jesus and also in the apostolic interpretation of the christological divine history. We must briefly examine both aspects.

New Testament scholars do not doubt that the use of the name "Father" by Jesus of Nazareth expressed an essential emphasis of his belief in God. It is true that the Father motif, as already indicated, was nothing new in the history of religion or in the age of Jesus. In addition to the examples given, we might cite others from the tradition of Judaism. Yet Jesus gave the name "Father" a distinctive point or turn. With full emphasis the word "Father" in the Gospels brings to the fore the motifs of special and almost tender nearness, and of a relation of love and trust.

In contrast, the patriarchal and authoritarian elements that are often associated with the word are in the background. We need to take note of the original Aramaic. The address used by Jesus was *Abba*. This is a childlike and familiar diminutive. In Greek it would be *pappa* rather than *pater*. How are we to understand this use? Not in terms of theological infantilism or sloppy fraternizing with God. The same Jesus of Nazareth could also speak of the absolute sovereignty and majesty of the Father. The Apostles' Creed looks in the same direction when it ties to the name "Father" the unmistakable predicate "Almighty." As we see from other sayings of Jesus which set children very close to the kingdom of God (Mark 10:15), we are to understand *Abba* in the sense of covenant faithfulness and trust. In the witness of Jesus this relation binds the Father unconditionally to his children, come what may.

Joachim Jeremias studied the word *Abba* in the sayings and prayers of Jesus and came to what is for me the convincing conclusion that it expresses in a special way something that is unique to Jesus. Jeremias argued that Jesus' message is without analogy—there is no parallel for the authority which dares to address God as *Abba*. Those who acknowledge the fact that Jesus himself used the term *Abba*, if they do not render the term innocuous, stand before the claim of Jesus to majesty. Those who read the parable of the prodigal son, which belongs to the bedrock of the tradition, and note that in this parable, which depicts the inconceivable forgiving kindness of God, Jesus is justifying his own table fellowship with tax collectors and sinners, also stand before the claim of Jesus to act as the representative and plenipotentiary of God.[3]

Apostolic christology is also involved—this is the second aspect of the New Testament use of the name "Father" for God. This christology set the central motif of Jesus' message concern-

---

3. Cf. Jeremias, *Prayers of Jesus*, e.g., pp. 29ff., 52ff., 96-98; idem, *Abba. Studien zur neutestamentlichen Theologie und Zeitgeschichte* (Göttingen: Vandenhoeck & Ruprecht, 1966); idem, "Der gegenwärtige Stand der Debatte um das Problem des historischen Jesus," in H. Ristow and K. Matthiae, eds., *Der historische Jesus und der kerygmatische Christus* (Berlin: 1960), p. 23.

ing God in the light of the Easter event, thus filling it out with the whole history and destiny of Jesus of Nazareth, and literally giving it flesh and blood. The self-giving of the Father to his children was factually and not just verbally unconditional. It was valid even unto death, and indeed beyond. The cross and resurrection fixed the divine location—better, they defined the divine nature. *Ecce Pater*—in New Testament terms it is the God of the cross and the resurrection that we see. The apostolic message bears witness to this God, this Father, the Father of Jesus Christ, as the New Testament again formulates it.

The simple name "Father," then, carries with it the whole revolution in the concept of God which is linked to the message and especially to the destiny of Jesus Christ: Immanuel, the God of faithful nearness in the deepest, most binding, and truly unconditional sense, in the sense of his incarnation, his identification with sons and daughters in life and death and to all eternity; God not merely in the height of his heavenly but also in the depths of his earthly course.

We have every reason to bring out the implications of this revolution in our theological work. More than ever today fidelity and conformity to the specific New Testament term "Father" are theologically important. For without them theologians easily fall victim to authoritarian and patriarchal concepts of God. The history of dogma shows how often such tendencies are present in the christologically unclarified concept of Father. A good part of prior history has stood under the sign of patriarchate, of an order of society controlled by fathers. Similarly, supreme gods have had authoritarian features as heavenly powers, rulers, "cosmopolicists." The history of Christian theology has been influenced by this tradition as well.

The patriarchal understanding of the divine name "Father" was always a serious misunderstanding. Today it is culturally fatal. For the age of authoritarian patriarchalism and paternalism is, we hope, over, whether in state or society. A patriarchal concept of God is doubly unbelievable.

Reflection on the christological anchoring of the apostolic term "Father" is, then, doubly important. The Father of Jesus

Christ is a wholly nonpatriarchal Father. The passage from Jeremias points already to the parable of the prodigal son, which is especially relevant in this context. We have only to note the figure of the father in the story. Against all prevailing laws and customs he does not stand in his son's way but lets him go, even though it is a highly risky and misconceived freedom that the younger son chooses. And when the prodigal returns crushed, the father does not count up and expect repayment but runs to meet him. The father runs: an unheard-of action in the patriarchal code. But this unheard-of feature in the father's attitude characterizes the New Testament concept. It cuts right across all pagan and pseudo-Christian ideas of God. As Helmut Gollwitzer points out, we must not, under Freud's influence, view the biblical Father-sayings as ties to a strict superego. The biblical title symbolizes God's preceding and life-giving turning to us to bring us home.[4] This Father who meets us nonjudgmentally is not an extension of the patriarchal and authoritarian mentality and order, but a challenge to it.

The existential and cosmic implications of belief in God the Father have been very impressively brought out by thinkers who have pondered and experienced the loss of it, even to its nihilistic implications. I have in mind especially Jean Paul (Richter) and his address of the dead Christ from the cosmic structure on the theme that there is no God. We have here a terrifying vision, an apocalyptic graveyard scene. The awakened dead cry out: "Christ, is there no God?" Christ takes up the question and tells of his wanderings through the wastes of heaven and the depths of the abyss in search of God the Father: "Father, where art thou?" But he hears only the eternal storm that no one controls, and the world stares at him, not with the divine eye of the Father but with an empty and bottomless eye socket. Then the dead children rush to him and cry out in despair: "Jesus, have we no Father?" And he answers with streaming tears: "We are all orphans, you and I; we are without a Father." All that re-

4. Helmut Gollwitzer, *Krummes Holz—aufrechter Gang* (Munich: 1970), p. 71.

mains is cold, eternal necessity and meaningless chance. What is especially terrifying is that the wounds that are inflicted in earthly life are never closed in any eternity, in any heaven. "Unhappy ones, they will not be closed after death." The general conclusion is that we are all alone in the vast crypt of the universe: "I am on my own."[5]

We must not misunderstand these moving statements. For Jean Paul this was dreaming truth, not waking truth. He was saying: God be thanked, this is not so. He opposed to it the waking truth, the truth of the Father, who embraces a glad, perishable world with his Son.[6] This truth is the more liberating the more closely he tested the alternative nightmare to the bitter end. If we can all be our own God and Creator, why cannot we also be our own angel of death? As in a reverse mirror we see here how little we can take the New Testament concept of the Father for granted, how easily we might contest it in an hour of temptation, but also how redemptive it is.

Heaven for Us

It is to this Father that Jesus addressed his prayer. On this point not only Matthew and Luke but also the rest of the New Testament agree. The one who is invoked is not left vague. He is the Father, the Lord who is revealed in the person and history of Jesus, the God of the covenant, the God of Israel. To the common factor Matthew adds two more precise extensions which we must now consider. In distinction from Luke he refers to the "Father in heaven" (literally, "in the heavens"). We can understand this expression in terms of his specific usage. He likes the words "heaven" and "heavenly." How often he speaks of "the kingdom of heaven." He is not attempting to specify a geographical location of the presence of God. To Jews of Jesus' time

5. Jean Paul (Richter), *Sämtliche Werke*, 1/6 (Weimar: 1928), pp. 247ff.
6. Cf. Gollwitzer, *Krummes Holz*, p. 106.

it was not self-evident that God dwelled in the heavens. Rather, they linked the place of his special presence to Zion and its temple, while for the Samaritans his dwelling was on Mount Gerizim. Basically, the disciples held aloof from that controversy—for reasons that are pointedly made clear in the Johannine dialog of Jesus with the Samaritan woman (John 4). God is the Father in heaven. If he once pledged himself to dwell on Zion or Sinai, on mountains or in the desert, he does so no more. The space in which a people lives and dwells with its God has been burst wide open, to be replaced by the incommensurability of heaven.[7]

Thus understood, the Matthean addition does not entail any metaphysical localizing of God (e.g., above the earth, as though astronauts could draw closer to him). Nor does it entail his greater distance, his transfer to an infinitely remote sphere. In Jesus the kingdom of heaven has come near to all of us (Matt. 4:17). The biblical term "heaven" expresses the absolute superiority of God to all visible and palpable reality, especially to our own reality and to the reality that we can grasp. Along the lines of Ephesians 3:15 and 4:6 we are to think of the sovereignty of God over all created things (over *panta* and *pantes*). But we are also to think of what results from this sovereignty, of his creative and liberating nearness to all, especially to believers.

This point sheds light on the simple but very important word "our": "Our Father." With this word Jesus resists any attempt to make the prayer a purely private matter. The temptation is a big one both outwardly and inwardly, both in past times and in present. Do not people in both East and West argue that religion is a private concern? No one can forbid us to pray, but it is our own business. And we are inwardly inclined to argue along the same lines: My prayer life (or its absence) is no one else's business. The little word "our" challenges this privatizing attitude. Certainly we are not encouraged to make a demonstration of prayer. The context of the Sermon on the Mount emphatically rules out this approach. But the spirit of the prayer of

7. See E. Lohmeyer, *"Lord's Prayer,"* pp. 60-61.

Jesus—even though we pray it in the quiet of our own room—bursts through the narrow circle of the pious *I*, resists all isolationism, and brings the *Thou* of others with it before the *Thou* of the Father.

Leonhard Ragaz stressed especially the importance of "our" in his exposition of the Lord's Prayer. The prayer, he said, is not an egotistic religious prayer but a social kingdom prayer. It is not an *I* prayer but a *We* prayer. It is not a prayer for me but a prayer for us. If we come before God in true prayer, we do not simply come before the God who is our private God but before the God who is the God of us all. He is the God who gathers us together with all his children, with our brothers and sisters. Thus the Lord's Prayer is the profoundest basis of true socialism.[8]

This does not mean the absorption of the praying *I* into a collective *We*. Biblically, prayer is conceivable only in personal responsibility. The *I* is particularly awake in prayer; we need think only of the "I" of the Psalms, but the same is true in the New Testament, as always in the practice of Jesus himself. Ragaz had a proper appreciation of this point, as he made clear: "You are for the first time genuinely alone when you pray to God. Before him you are in the right against the whole world. In him and only in him you are free. God is not a God of the masses, of collectives, of herds of people. In prayer Jesus opposes the Grand Inquisitor. From prayer comes the saying that we are to obey God rather than men."[9] But awake in this way, we must be free to look out for our neighbors. "Mass man" does not become "superman" but the "Lord's man"—the New Testament "man of the Lord" who is free to tread the way of the Lord, the child of the Father.

We are to think of the motif of the children of God in this regard. It is undoubtedly echoed in the invocation as a correlate of the name "Father." The Synoptics, it is true, do not use the term "children of God." Matthew and Luke speak only of the

8. Leonhard Ragaz, "Das Unservater," in *Von der Revolution der Bibel* (Zurich: 1943), 1:9.

9. Ibid.

"sons of God," and they do so only in the future sense of eschatological promise. Yet with impressive clarity the Fourth Gospel
sums up in the designation "children of God" the quintessence
of eschatological salvation and the expression of God's fatherly
love (John 1:13; 3:3, 5, 6-8; cf. also 1 John 2:29; 3:9; 4:7; 5:1, 4-18).[10]
That this is not just a Johannine specialized use but a reflection
of a basic conviction of the disciples and the primitive community (along the lines of the Lord's Prayer) may be seen from Paul
when he quite naturally links the cry "Abba, Father" to the description of believers as the sons or children of God.

What does the expression "children (or sons) of God"
mean? It might perhaps be misunderstood today as implying a
Christian infantilism or immaturity. This sense would be suspect, especially in the "century of the child." But the New Testament use points in a very different direction. We have to remember that the clearest apostolic references relate to it the promise
of freedom and maturity. I have in mind Galatians 4, where
God's liberating movement in the sending of his Son aims at the
mature freedom of the children of God: "And because you are
sons, God has sent the Spirit of his Son into our hearts, crying,
'Abba, Father!' So through God you are no longer a slave but a
son, and if a son then an heir" (4:6-7). There is no doubt that sonship is the opposite of slavery and immaturity here. Similarly,
in Romans 8, that great chapter of hope, the cry "Abba, Father"
is seen as empowerment for freedom in the Spirit in the midst
of the bondage of corruption to which, to the sighing of all creation, everything created is subject.

None of this is self-evident. It involves the narrow way of
exodus and deliverance in virtue of sonship, a sonship that is
granted on the way of Jesus of Nazareth, also and above all in
his cross and resurrection. Being a child of God is not, then, a
common, ontologically given quality or *habitus* of the human
race. It has a concrete basis in the incarnate Son. It is thus concretely anchored. It is not a general matter but calls for a concrete response. This is made clear in the Johannine Prologue:

10. See Lohmeyer, *"Lord's Prayer,"* p. 49.

"He came to his own home, but his own people received him not. But to all who received him . . . he gave power to become children of God" (1:11ff.). This makes the *We* of the Lord's Prayer more precise. The emphatic subject of the prayer is not a blurred or cosmopolitan collective but the concrete fellowship of Christian brothers and sisters. Carrying forward the analogy of father and children, this fellowship influences the vocabulary of the New Testament and the church. To the Father on the vertical level correspond brothers and sisters on the horizontal level. The fact that in the early church the Lord's Prayer was not an open prayer, but the prayer of the baptized at the eucharist, underlines this understanding.

Is it then a sectarian matter? The separation of a holy group from an unholy world? Not at all. The unmistakably concrete basis of being a child of God in the person and history of Jesus of Nazareth breaks down from the outset all the barriers that devout and righteous sectarians finally want to erect around themselves. The path of Jesus was an initiative of loving solidarity aimed not only at the near but also at the distant, those written off by morality and religion. The exclusiveness of God's christocentric fatherhood, and of the sonship based upon it, develops an inclusive dynamic which seeks conformity in the mind and acts of Christians (cf. Phil. 2:1-5). "Christians who regard themselves as . . . good children of God, Christians who refuse to sit with their Master at the table of publicans and sinners, are *not* Christians at all, have still to become so, and need not be surprised if heaven is gray above them and their calling upon God sounds hollow and finds no hearing."[11] The fatherhood of God that is open to us in Christ kindles a correspondingly open sonship in Christians that strides across all frontiers. The little word "our," the *We* of the Lord's Prayer, is exclusively based but in this very fact it is an uncommonly inclusive word.

It is in this direction that the invocation of the Lord's Prayer points us in our living and praying. I will sum it all up in some words of Calvin: "Let the Christian man, then, conform

11. Barth, *Christian Life*, p. 80.

26

. his prayers to this rule in order that they may be in common and embrace all who are his brothers in Christ, not only those whom he at present sees and recognizes as such but all men who dwell on earth. For what God has determined concerning them is beyond our knowing except that it is no less godly than humane to wish and hope the best for them."[12]

12. Calvin, *Institutes*, 2:901, § 3.20.38.

Hallowed Be Thy Name

The Need and Necessity of God

It has always evoked astonishment and even alienation that the Lord's Prayer begins with the petition: "Hallowed be thy name." Even today people find this a relatively difficult petition compared to the others. When they do not find anything similar in the recorded sayings of Jesus, in his message as we have it in the Gospels, they think that no great prominence is given to the motif of hallowing God's name. It occurs comparatively seldom, and that mostly in Old Testament quotations. If we compare it with the next central motif, that of the kingdom of God, its place is marginal. Hence one might conclude that the heart of Jesus really begins to beat only when he comes to the second petition: "Thy kingdom come."

Again, compared to the other petitions, does not this first one seem rather flat to us? What are we to make of abstract sounding words like "name" and "hallowed" in the secularized world of today? To be sure, one might put the same question regarding the other petitions, but here at the outset the lack of relevance seems particularly great and therefore the chance of understanding particularly small as compared to what follows. It is no wonder that some have attempted to water down the meaning of the statement by not very convincingly regarding it as a continuation of the invocation and making "Thy kingdom come" the first true petition.

I am opposed to attempts and deliberations of this sort. If we orient ourselves generally to Scripture, we can hardly avoid the conclusion that this is very directly a petition that we need to make. Its place at the head of the prayer is not accidental; it has its basis in the very heart of the biblical outlook. In other words, it corresponds to what is biblically the one thing necessary, the human need (and necessity) of God. The plain cantus firmus in the polyphony of biblical witnesses, of the prophets and apostles, is the reference to God in acknowledgment and confession.

Clear though that may be to the biblical witnesses, is it clear to us? We need to show how far we can speak of a necessity or even a need of God (analogous to the necessity or need of food), though not in the sense of primary needs or of a logically present necessity. One might debate whether God is a universal human need. If much speaks in favor of it, and that not merely in the history of religion, much also speaks against it, and that not merely in the history of atheism. Human needs are ambivalent and changeable. Hence I would rather not speak of a need of God in that sense. And the attempt to declare an absolute necessity of God, as in (subjectively respectable) attempts at proofs of God in Western philosophy, is something that I would rather avoid in the present context. I also have reservations about the way in which Karl Jaspers speaks about the necessity of God in his categorical statement that only transcendence is real being, that if deity *is*, that is enough, and being certain of it is the one thing that matters.[1] In its way this is no doubt a fine and notable statement, but it is too categorical and general, hardly doing justice to the personal tension in the biblical theme of God.

It is not in the sense of a subjectively self-evident need nor in that of an objectively self-evident necessity that we are to un-

---

1. Karl Jaspers, "Über meine Philosophie" (1941), in *Rechenschaft und Ausblick* (1951), p. 345.

derstand the human need of God, but in that of the founding and preserving of true human freedom. In this connection I would like to adopt a brilliant and helpful saying of Eberhard Jüngel: "God is not necessary."[2] To say this is to bid farewell to the self-evident God, the God who from the very first is built into our prevailing view of the world, the God of the proofs insofar as they are more than acts of thinking faith seeking to understand itself and to give an account of itself, insofar as they aim to force people to acknowledge God by logic, to prove him to be necessary. It is to bid farewell also—and this is the essential practical result from the standpoint of cultural and social policy—to the obligatory God whom one can force on the minds and consciences of others with threats and sanctions. We must bid farewell to a self-evident God of this kind, not under the pressure of a changed age but in fresh consideration of the origin of faith. For the God of biblical faith is different. He is not necessary.

God is more than necessary. The correlate and counter-point of necessity is freedom. I believe that the biblical name of God has its setting in the history of the freedom of God's people. Here is the locus of revelation. In the Old Testament we think of the story of the exodus, the normative act of liberation for Israel. In the New Testament we have an indissoluble link to the Easter story. One of the most impressive apostolic defi-nitions of God is "he that raised from the dead Jesus our Lord" (Rom. 4:24). The name of God is proclaimed here in the context of the supreme event of freedom, of liberation from the last enemy, temporal and eternal death. At the heart of the Bible God is identical with the promise of life, of its invasion of the world of death.[3]

Third World theologians seem to have a sharper eye for this setting of the biblical theme of God than traditional West-ern theology. It is no accident that in a particularly emphatic

2. Eberhard Jüngel, *God as the Mystery of the World,* tr. Darrell L. Guder (Grand Rapids: Eerdmans, 1983), p. 16. Cf. my rectoral address "Im Namen Gottes des Allmächtigen," Basel, 1982, especially pp. 8ff.
3. See H. Gollwitzer, *Krummes Holz,* p. 284.

way they have worked out a theology of liberation, and done so with an intensity that makes us take notice. It is worth noting that not only Latin American but also African theologians have emphasized this aspect of liberation. This is undoubtedly connected with the absence of freedom under the conditions of colonial and racist government. Thus Allan Boesak in the South African situation can argue that freedom is not a mere part of the gospel, not one of the evangelical key words; it is the content and point of reference of the whole biblical message.[4] Such categorical statements are perhaps one-sided, but they point in the right direction. This theology is ecumenically convincing because from its own experience it very forcefully focuses attention on the biblically central themes of exodus and resurrection, and not least the theme of freedom. Only too often the biblically constitutive connection is concealed and relativized either objectivistically in the metaphysical tradition of the West or subjectivistically in the psychologizing present-day trend. There are good theological reasons why we should learn from the theology of liberation at this essential point, and not merely in social ethics.

The name of God has to do with this matter which is for us essential, that is, with the grounding and preserving of freedom in our human world. The petition "Hallowed be thy name" relates to this truly fundamental need. Is that weak and abstract? We are dealing here with our human condition. In many respects we human beings are creatures of necessity. We are dependent on nature, limited and shaped by our psychological makeup, entangled in complicated relations of culture and history, and conditioned by structures and pressures of economic and social destiny. Yet in fact are we only that? Hardly anyone who has self-awareness will agree that we are. We want to remain "we" in life and death. It is here that the Bible helps us. For all our recognition of the weight of necessity, naming the name of God sets something else in the scales. We are not just the human world ("the world of men," as Marx once put

4. Allan Boesak, *Farewell to Innocence* (New York: Orbis, 1977), p. 17.

31

it). We are more than an ensemble of social relationships. In the vivid language of the Bible, even though taken from earth and creatures of necessity, we are made in the image of God as children of freedom, related even in the midst of necessity to what is more than necessary. Here in our primal human situation we are set in the life of prayer which manifests a recognition of the incalculable dimension of human nature and our personal worth. Prayer expresses the fact that in the sphere of the necessary, of what can be planned and made, we are never fully calculable. Measures of production and achievement, which are meaningful in their place, are never adequate to establish or determine our human rights and worth. We are conditioned beings, but in God's sight we have unconditional dignity.

The petition "Hallowed be thy name" relates to this basic condition, to the need of God which is also our deepest need. It stands rightly at the head of the Lord's Prayer. Its hearing and fulfilling constitute the presupposition or, shall we say, create the free space in which the petitions that follow can also have their basis and meaning.

More than Sound and Smoke

If we set the wording of the first petition against the background of prayer life in Jesus' time, we may say that like the next two petitions it follows very closely the Kaddish, the closing prayer of synagogue worship that all Jewish children, certainly including Jesus, knew very well. I will quote what Joachim Jeremias thinks was its oldest form: "Exalted and hallowed be his great name in the world which he created according to his will. May he let his kingdom rule in your lifetime and in your days and in the lifetime of the whole house of Israel, speedily and soon. And to this, say: amen."[5] We should not overlook the fact that the Kaddish contains the first petition in full. This is theologically

5. Jeremias, *Prayers of Jesus,* p. 98.

important. We cannot separate the prayer of Jesus from the piety of his people. The Old Testament and Jewish background is of normative significance for its understanding.

We must pay attention to this background when we focus in detail on the two expressions in the petition. To Old Testament and Jewish ears the petition was anything but flat. The two expressions address two decisive elements in the faith and thought of Israel. This is true first of the name. Today it is hard for most of us to grasp the significance of the name, especially the name of God. In this regard our preconception is nominalistic. It belongs to a form of thinking which regards names and words as conventional means of expression and instruments of communication. It differs from the thought-forms of the philosophy of classical antiquity, especially Platonic philosophy, which ascribed high value to concepts and names and which the Middle Ages called realist in distinction from the later nominalists. Many of us could agree at this point with Goethe, when in his *Faust,* answering the question regarding God, he wrote that we might call the deity fortune, heart, love, or God, there is no name for it, feeling is everything, name is sound and smoke, a cloud-girt heavenly glow.

The Bible takes a different view. For it the name is much more than a conventional and arbitrary utterance, sound and smoke. It carries with it the mystery of the unique personality of its bearer. In many important cases it announces a whole life-program. In biblical thinking *nomen est omen* and much more, for it stands for the inalienable and uncontrollable nature and presence of personal reality. This explains the typical reverence for the name, and very emphatically and incomparably for the name of God. We need think only of the third commandment: "You shall not take the name of the Lord your God in vain, for the Lord will not hold him guiltless who takes his name in vain" (Exod. 20:7).

It is surprising how closely God and his name are linked, especially in the Old Testament, where they are even interchangeable. "Behold, the name of the Lord comes from far, burning with his anger, and in thick rising smoke; his lips are full of indignation, and his tongue is like a devouring fire" (Isa. 30:27). "So they shall fear the name of the Lord from the west, and his glory from the rising of the sun; for he will come like a rushing stream, which the wind of the Lord drives" (Isa. 59:19). So, too, in the New Testament: "For God is not so unjust as to overlook your work and the love which you showed for his name in serving the saints, as you still do" (Heb. 6:10). The striking closeness of God to his name, and the possibility of making both the subjects of the one saving act, make it plain that the name is not just a secondary quality of God, or an additional predicate, or a cipher that one may change at will. It has to do with the very nature of God. Indeed, one might put it even more strongly: God *is* his name. Abraham Calov, a representative of post-Reformation orthodoxy, stated along these lines that the name of God is God himself, and from the biblical standpoint he was right. In this respect two special motifs are connected with the express naming of the name of God. It makes known his sovereign personality and the fact that he is revealed. The name denotes the manifest personal presence of God both in heaven and on earth.

We need to have a lively sense of the relevance of the name as thus understood, of its reference to actual life. Is not the supremely real problem of our age the growing anonymity and the related depersonalizing of our life-style? The danger is not new, but it is coming to a head in technological-industrial civilization with its material pressures, and especially in our computer age, which is tempted to reduce more and more of human life to data, if not indeed to manipulate it.

In his exposition of the Lord's Prayer Walter Lüthi drew attention to the liberating way in which our petition opposes nameless processes and powers. He pointed out that "God has a name. The misery on this earth is nameless, the evil among men is nameless, for the powers of darkness love to be without a name. Nameless, anonymous letters, letters without signatures are usually vulgar. But God is no writer of anonymous letters; God puts His name to everything that He does, effects, and

34

says; God has no need to fear the light of day. The Devil loves anonymity, but God has a name."[6]

The petition resists anonymity. It resists the temptation to reduce humanity to impersonal processes, to subject it to totalitarianism, whether technocratic or ideological. It does so by reminding us of the sovereign, personal name of God. The Old Testament revelation of God's name is as follows: "I am who I am" (Exod. 3:14). This is puzzling at first, but it is not a mystical riddle about which one can endlessly speculate. It is a reference to the fact that we cannot control God or manipulate him. He cannot be grasped magically. He has turned to his people in person with the promise of his name: "I will be there for you" (as we might render the Hebrew). Immanuel, God with us, is also the meaning of God's name in the New Testament, concretely fulfilled by the name and history of Jesus Christ. It is no accident that in Matthew the whole story is seen and interpreted in terms of this name (Matt. 1:23).

The prayer reminds us of this name, and in so doing it protects our personal humanity. Isaiah expressed this in unforgettable words: "Fear not, for I have redeemed you; I have called you by name, you are mine. When you pass through the waters, I will be with you; and through the rivers, they shall not overwhelm you . . . For I am the Lord (Yahweh) your God, the Holy One of Israel, your Savior" (Isa. 43:1-3). It was when Israel was in a difficult political situation that this promise was given to the people, but it is still valid for us today as we pass through our own waters and fiery trials. For when God has given his name and remains faithful to it—the name Immanuel—we, too, are given a lasting name, the identity which is grounded by God and before God and which is inalienable in spite of all determinations to the contrary. We, too, have our names. We *are* our names. We do not dissolve into namelessness. Before God we are inexchangeable. We live and die with our irrevocable human right.

6. W. Lüthi, *The Lord's Prayer: An Exposition*, tr. Kurt Schoenenberger (Richmond, VA: John Knox, 1961), p. 10.

This promise has a distinctive, liberating effect. If our names have right and validity before God, we are not forced to make a name for ourselves at all costs, which is an only too human temptation. Near the beginning of the Bible this was the delusion of those who built the tower of Babel (Gen. 11). Their motive for building "a tower with its top to the heavens" was this: "Let us make a name for ourselves" (v. 4). But trees and towers never reach to heaven. The dream of a great name is a tragic illusion and snare (which often ends in tragicomedy). We need think only of the dreams of Babel's arrogance. Along similar lines, many have more modest daydreams, such as the search for an image in everyday life. What will people not do to make a name for themselves, to achieve distinction, to make themselves different from others, often at others' cost! They do this at every level. Image seems more important than reality. But often a name in this sense, logically enough, becomes nothing more than sound and smoke, having no substance, and being lost only too quickly.

Recollection of the name of God—Immanuel—saves us from such daydreams and nightmares. We need not exert ourselves to make a name for ourselves, for the name of God is there for us, we have our own names before God, and indeed we are these names, unique persons. "Your names are written in heaven" (Luke 10:20). In the first apostolic preaching in Acts the heart of the confession is this: "There is no other name under heaven given among men by which we must be saved" (Acts 4:12). It is sobering and yet also comforting to know that other names do not save. Above all, my own name does not save. We do not stand or fall by the greatness of our name. We stand (and do not fall) by the greatness of the name of God. Freed, then, from the compulsion and delusion of those who would make a name, in the liberty of those who are called children of God, we pray: "Hallowed be thy name."

Zeal for the Honor of God

The name of God, God himself, the "Father" of the Lord's Prayer, is to be hallowed. It is important to state that the transition from one of the two motifs of the first petition to the other calls for no great leap. The two motifs are biblically very close to one another. The name of God plays a special role in Isaiah. But the same Isaiah is also the great witness to the holiness of God. His irresistible encounter with God at his calling stands under the sign of an overpowering (triune) holiness which comes to expression in the cry of the seraphim: "Holy, holy, holy is the Lord of hosts" (Isa. 6:3). Like the name of God, the holiness of God has to do with his personal being. It is no accident that the two motifs come together in expressions like "the holy name." God and holiness belong inseparably together in the Bible.

What is the emphasis of the thrice-holy of Isaiah? Alluding to this passage we might say, with Lohmeyer, that "Holiness here is what makes God God, the incomprehensible ground of his being, the hidden essence of which no one even begins to be aware, which he reveals only as it pleases him. There is no rest here; even this final essence is action in the twofold sense of activity and actuality, and whatever he does is a revelation of what is hidden."[7] It is in keeping with this that in both the Old Testament and the New there is a close, one might say a dialectical, relation between holiness and glory. As Oetinger put it, "God's revealed holiness is his glory, his holiness is his hidden glory."[8]

To get closer to the standpoint of the first petition it will be worth our while to think of Johannine usage. I have already remarked that the Synoptics do not use the terms of the petition much, but that they are more common in the Johannine writings, and stand out sharply in the prayers of Jesus: "Holy Father keep them in thy name, which thou hast given me" (John 17:11). Again, along the lines of the dialectic of holiness and glory: "Father, glorify thy name" (12:28). Note that in all these petitions

---

7. Lohmeyer, *"Lord's Prayer,"* p. 72.
8. Quoted in ibid.

for the hallowing or glorifying of the name of God, Jesus is looking unmistakably in the one direction, namely, at the Father, at God himself. It is to God that he addresses the petition. God himself is primarily the subject of the hallowing of his name.

I stress this orientation because many expositions of the Lord's Prayer, though not overlooking it, have often dealt with it too summarily. The fathers and even the Reformation catechisms moved quickly to attempts to impress upon us Christians the task (usually moral) of hallowing the name of God. This transition is in fact necessary; indeed, it is indispensable. It is true to the Bible itself, for the witness to God's holiness himself points to the transition when he states: "Be holy, for I am holy" (Lev. 11:44; 19:2; 20:26). One might call this link the basis of Old Testament piety, and the New Testament adopts it as well, as in 1 Peter 1:16, and indeed in the familiar saying of Jesus himself in the Sermon on the Mount: "You, therefore, must be perfect, as your heavenly Father is perfect" (Matt. 5:48). There is no doubt that the transition to the practical implications must be made, but as a transition, not as the first thing. What is primary is the petition, addressed to God, that he would hallow his own name.

This is the right sequence. Why? Because if not, we do not do justice to the seriousness of our own unholy alienation. Karl Barth dealt expressly and very forcefully with this question in his discussion of the first petition under the fine title "Zeal for the Honor of God." He found the setting for the prayer in the bitter experience of the permanent desecration of the name of God in the world. The most common and basic form of this desecration is the notorious ambivalence with which we who are already addressed and sought and saved by God nevertheless take so little account of God our Creator and Savior in our lives. This may be seen in our attitudes and relationships in the world, especially in our contacts with other people, in the fact that "man can be important to man, a neighbor, friend, and helper, and yet at any moment indifferent, a stranger, enemy, and corrupter . . . more a wolf than a person. . . . If we wish to know what is the true and final point of the petition 'Hallowed be thy name' . . . then we had better focus our attention on this one thing, on the evil fact that we humans . . . can be and are both everything and nothing to one another, both fellow men and wolves."[9]

Even our life in the church displays a similar ambivalence. But here, since God's yes is known with special clarity in the church, it is even more critical. Here the light of God's name that is entrusted to us is darkened, and mostly, unfortunately, by the church itself. Barth points out that there are two forms of failure in the church. There is that of excess in which the church is self-conscious and self-satisfied, curving in upon itself, pretending to be the representative of the kingdom of God. There is also that of deficiency. The church does not take itself seriously enough, venturing to confess its task in too timid and uncommitted a fashion, making up for its little faith by substitute activities. It is a distracted church, a chattering, squinting, stuttering church— in a word, a secularized church.

There is also division in personal life. This is not to be confused with the experience that in our faith we are always on the way and never at the goal, pilgrims and not owners. Sober recognition of this condition is part of Christian existence. What is not part of it is our cultivated lack of commitment, our relaxed vacillation between possibilities, our refusal to venture an unequivocal yes or no. This is desecration of God's name as it is practiced in the lives of Christians. "This vacillation or neutrality in which Christians can be and are one thing or the other, thinking, speaking, and doing one thing or the other, is the monstrosity."[10] We must resist this. Prayer is a mobilizing for resistance, a summons to it. "The wakeful church and its wakeful members pray 'Hallowed be thy name' even though all around them . . . there continues the apathetic and monotonous murmur: 'At one and the same time both righteous and sinner, world without end. Amen.'"[11]

9. Barth, *Christian Life,* p. 132.
10. Ibid., p. 150.
11. Ibid., p. 154.

All these various tendencies in the world, the church, and personal life accumulate and mount up into what Barth describes as the regime of vacillation, division, and obfuscation. Even our best will is not a match for this compact conglomerate. As Luther rightly saw, "With force of arms we nothing can, Full soon were we down-ridden." These lines are more apt than devout sighing. The sober experience of history teaches us that efforts to escape the ambivalence of the human heart and condition by ethical and political power, for all the good intentions, lead only to tragic reverses. Think of the political attempts to set up an ideal society by force, or of sympathetic but in the long run overhasty attempts to set up an ideal church, the commonwealth of saints, the realized kingdom of God on earth. Think, too, of the constant failures of perfectionists who have claimed too much for themselves and others, imagining that they could reach Christian perfection this side of the kingdom of God. Such efforts possibly begin in genuine zeal for the honor of God, but all of them are perverted sooner or later into a sectarian and destructive fanaticism. Let us take heed!

Shall we then capitulate? Shall we reconcile ourselves to unholy relations in the world, the church, and our own lives? Shall we compromise? Shall we accept the state of ambivalence as permanent and normal? Realists of all stripes incline to this conclusion. People and the world, they say, will never change. But this realism can never be our strategy so long as we take the petition "Hallowed be thy name" seriously, and pray it seriously. For if the prayer certainly has in view the common experience of dominant ambivalence in our human world, it will not let us be silent in face of it, but summons us in the name of the one counterforce that comes into question here, the name of Almighty God. This was how the prophets and apostles reacted to hopeless situations. They did not adjust but appealed to the holy name of God. We again quote Isaiah: "O that thou wouldst rend the heavens and come down, that the mountain might quake at thy presence . . . to make thy name known to thy adversaries, and that the nations might tremble at thy presence" (64:1-2).

This is not a confession of the power of one's own ideals, or a declaration of trust in the force of one's own moral and political battalions. It is an appeal to the power and faithfulness of God, that he will make a breach in the regime of ambivalence and desecration, that he will make good his promises, that he will create the needed space for us and our efforts at hallowing his name. Only with his intervention can we really overcome the tragic temptation of pride and apostasy or sloth and dissipation. I venture to say that in this sense the prayer is the real and true answer to the real state of things in our human world. Faust was wrong to find deed in the beginning. John was right: "In the beginning was the Word, and the Word was with God." We are to pray and work, but the law of praying is the law of working. This is the proper order.

Yet in this order we have to take the second part seriously, the working and the law of working. If in a titanic self-understanding our action might betray a tragic misunderstanding of human conditions, nevertheless, it is not only possible but necessary as an active response to the Word and the deed of God. The petition for the hallowing of God's name is addressed to God but it also engages those who pray it. The inner structure of the biblical motif of holiness points unmistakably in this direction. We recall again the Old Testament command: "Be holy, for I am holy." The one thing involves the other. On the Reformation view the order of salvation sets justification and sanctification in this sequence, but it also perceives that within this sequence they are inseparably related. As I would see it, sanctification without justification would be blind, but justification without sanctification would be empty. The petition for the hallowing of God's name mobilizes us against such a vacuum.

In the history of exposition, and precisely in the Reformation catechisms, this aspect, as I have already indicated, receives special emphasis. Appeal is often made to the statement of Augustine: "When we say, Hallowed be thy name, we are admonishing ourselves to consider that his name, which is eternally holy, should be kept holy among us, i.e., that it should not be disdained."

41

No Double Christian Life

Disdain for God's name is an everyday occurrence. It is displayed always, everywhere, and by all, as the Christian doctrine of sin, under the title "original sin," rightly stresses with reference to the universal enslavement of the human race under the regime of sin. If in the New Testament, in the light of the story of Jesus, the name of God finds its supreme fulness in the name "love" ("God is love," 1 John 4:8), then desecration of the name of God is to be understood above all as lovelessness, the forms of which largely characterize everyday life, on both a big scale and a small, in the world, the church, and the individual.

Desecration of God's name is thus a universal phenomenon among us. Yet it is particularly acute as the problem of the church, of the Christian life. Desecration of the holy is an abomination in both the Old Testament and the New. But the people of God, Israel and Christians, can be addressed as holy. Thus the petition to hallow the name of God is particularly applicable to them. The praying *I* and the praying *We* are questioned in this regard, and question themselves. In what sense?

Recalling the Decalog can be a help to understanding. I have mentioned already that the first petition bears a striking resemblance to the third commandment: "You shall not take the name of the Lord your God in vain." This warning and the prayer for the hallowing of God's name obviously correspond to one another. What does the Decalog mean by taking God's name in vain? Primarily it has in view the attempt to acquire magical or priestly control over the name (the church in excess). It also has in view carelessness and caprice in dealing with God and his Word and instability in the question of truth (the church in defect). In addition, we have to think of a specific temptation of the people of God to refuse discipleship. The name of God, the name of Jesus Christ, is recognized and named, but what it stands for is not taken seriously. There is an appeal to the gospel or to the confession, but no commitment to it, no acceptance of its implications. People say "Lord, Lord" but do not do the Lord's will. The commission of the church and the lives of Christians thus lose credibility. They cease to be an instrument for the hallowing of God's name in the world and become instead an obstacle to it.[12]

The first petition of the Lord's Prayer calls upon God and rouses the church steadfastly to resist this type of Christian confusion, this regime of division, or, as I would rather say, to put an end to this unbelievability, and to cause the holy and healing name of God to shine out more clearly in credible word and service. This is the basic determination and goal of Christianity. In this determinative sense, the first petition lays the foundation for all that follows. Rightly, then, it comes at the head of the Lord's Prayer: "Hallowed be thy name."

The Caribbean has given us a musical version of the Lord's Prayer which is often sung enthusiastically in the ecumenical movement (Philip Potter especially likes it). It consists of the simple biblical text but puts "Hallowed be thy name" after every petition. For many years I never thought about this, but it now seems to me that the repetition is not just a chance result of music and poetry but carries with it a theological emphasis and clarification. First and last, as the concluding doxology shows, what is at issue in prayer and action is the hallowing of God's name. As the Reformation catechisms, especially those of Reformed provenance, stress constantly, the vital goal of human life is to glorify God (cf. Geneva and Westminster). The longing that from the center of our lives, for all our human weakness, God should be hallowed, God should be credibly glorified, is basic to the Reformation, and indeed to the ecumenical heritage: "Hallowed be thy name."

A concluding note concerning the catchword "ecumenical." In his exposition of the Lord's Prayer, Lohmeyer pointed out that the first petition has an eschatological, ecumenical, missionary dimension. "The idea of the hallowing of God's name points to an eschatological act before which all historical differences of peoples and languages vanish and in which at the same

---

12. Cf. my work *Signposts to Freedom: The Ten Commandments and Christian Ethics,* tr. David Lewis (Minneapolis: Augsburg, 1982), pp. 52-56.

time the world is presupposed as a well ordered and 'sanctified' entity. So it is understandable that this first petition has become so to speak the petition for the mission to the Gentiles. Just as Ps. 86:9 says: 'All the nations thou hast made shall come and bow down before thee, O Lord, and shall glorify thy name.'"[13] Undoubtedly, the impulse behind the petition is ecumenical and missionary, crossing all frontiers. Its field is the world, its horizon the kingdom of God.

13. Lohmeyer, "Lord's Prayer," pp. 85-86.

Thy Kingdom Come

Loving Earth and God in One

Dietrich Bonhoeffer pointed out that people today, being either otherworldly or secularists, no longer believe in God's kingdom. They are either hostile to the earth because they want to be better than it is, or hostile to God because he deprives us of the earth our mother. They either flee from the power of the earth or cling firmly and immovably to it. They are not "wanderers who love the earth that carries them, yet love it only because in it they meet the foreign land that they love above all things, since otherwise they would not be wanderers. Only those who wander thus, who love earth and God in one, can believe in the kingdom of God."[1]

These words of Bonhoeffer, which come from a church address in 1932, describe one of the problem areas in which the central theme of God's kingdom is placed today for the Christian community and its theology. The dialectic that is constitutive for this biblical theme can be threatened or dissolved in two ways. With innumerable variations both possibilities have been tried in church history. We can understand God's kingdom

---

1. Bonhoeffer, "Dein Reich komme," in *Gesammelte Schriften* (Munich: Kaiser, 1960), 3:270.

as an absolutely otherworldly reality, as a transcendent "hinter-world." To our pious gaze earth grows pale and finally becomes insignificant, unworthy of pious words or pious deeds. The kingdom of God has to do not with the labyrinth of the world but with the paradise of the heart. It is to this that we must flee from earthly disillusionments and pressures.

One can understand this piety of otherworldliness and in-wardness. In some situations in earthly life, individual and so-cial, the pressure of relations or the burden of anxieties becomes so strong that one thinks one can find in this way a certain tran-scendent comfort in comfortless experiences. Such comfort is easily had and is everywhere available. When life begins to get painful or obtrusive, said Bonhoeffer, we make a bold leap into the air and rise up lightly and unhampered into so-called eter-nal fields.[2] But we must not confuse this trampoline exercise with belief in the kingdom of God. It is more like religion as Marx described it in his well-known saying that religion is the sign of the oppressed creature, the heart of a heartless world, the spirit of spiritless conditions. It is the opiate of the people.[3]

The opposite extreme to the otherworldly tendency in un-derstanding God's kingdom is the secularist tendency. This time the earth is not betrayed. Earthly relations and Christian re-sponsibility for shaping them are taken seriously. Efforts are made to do kingdom-work, and at times there are notable achievements along these lines, which we have to appreciate. The secularist temptation is present when consciously or uncon-sciously God's kingdom is equated with specific earthly ends and the kingdom reaches its goal in the rule of the church. We ourselves build up God's kingdom. We are architects of God's future as well as our own. Our plans and achievements are thus sanctified. The kingdom of God does not come; we come into the kingdom.

Such tendencies are especially present in the modern

2. Ibid.

3. Marx, *Die Frühschriften,* ed. S. Landshut (Stuttgart: Kröner, 1953), p. 208.

church, often in truly attractive movements run by Christians who are culturally and socially alert. I have in mind the varied trends in cultural forms of Protestantism or religious-social movements. Their input is to be highly valued, but what is often their shortsighted grounding of the idea of the kingdom of God is an occasion for criticism.

I will mention one particularly clear example, the American Social Gospel movement. It is the lasting merit of this movement that it vigorously set in the center of theoretical and practical attention the social dimension of the Christian message and Christian responsibility. As Walter Rauschenbusch said, the kingdom of God is a precious truth, the center of the gospel as the incarnation was for Athanasius, justification for Luther, and the sovereignty of God for Jonathan Edwards.[4] Yet prominent in the kingdom of God according to the Social Gospel (and its leading theologian Rauschenbusch) was a troublesome ambiguity. The kingdom of God approximated very closely to a program for the progressive christianizing of secular orders in modern society. In this sense Rauschenbusch (in 1912!) could see and proclaim great fulfilments of the kingdom of God in American civilization. After the christianizing of family, church, school, and state, the only remaining area to be tackled was the economic sphere. In this case the motif of the kingdom has undoubtedly undergone wide-ranging but shortsighted secularization.

We must avoid the two dead ends on the path to an understanding of the petition "Thy kingdom come"—the private dead end and the overhasty social dead end. We must agree with Bonhoeffer's summary statement that the prayer for the kingdom is not the begging of an anxious soul for blessedness nor is it Christian embellishment for world-improvers. It is the prayer of the suffering and warring community in the world for the human race and for the fulfilling of God's glory in it.[5] What is this third way of understanding the petition? What is a re-

4. Rauschenbusch, *A Theology for the Social Gospel* (Nashville: Abingdon, repr. 1981), p. 131.
5. Bonhoeffer, *Gesammelte Schriften*, 3:278.

sponsible definition of the relation between the reality of God and our earthly reality?

In the first passage from Bonhoeffer we twice find the motif of wandering. But this wandering, we are told, corresponds to God's kingdom only when the wanderer loves earth and God in one. From the standpoint of the kingdom of God and its goal, the motif of wandering reminds me of something in church history which is very dear to me, the Czech Reformation. Here an orientation to God's kingdom in both the personal and the social sense played an important role—much more so than in the sixteenth-century Reformation—from beginning to end.

I will mention just two examples. At the beginning was the father of the Czech Reformation, Jan Milíč from Kroměříž. This powerful preacher, with strong eschatological and apocalyptic emphases, founded in the center of Prague an institution where those on the margin of society, the outcasts of the Middle Ages, former prostitutes, might seek refuge. To the annoyance of the righteous and self-righteous, he called this institution New Jerusalem. He was not, of course, equating God's heavenly city with existing social relations, for how could he equate it with a group that most people despised? Critically and in hope, however, he was making a connection. The heavenly city of God has to do with the hard pavements of our cities. Hope of the kingdom must be practiced in earthly relations. In Bonhoeffer's words, we are to love earth and God in one.

This was also the confession of the last great thinker of the Czech Reformation, Jan Amos Comenius. Comenius was literally and painfully a wanderer. For most of his life he was a refugee. As he said, "My life was a wandering; I had no home. I was restlessly and unceasingly cast hither and thither; nowhere and never did I find a place to settle. But now I see already my heavenly homeland."[6] Yet this wandering to a heavenly goal, this way from "the labyrinth of the world to the paradise of the heart" (the title of one of his best-known works), was not a private flight. It involved an almost inconceivably varied striving

6. Comenius, *Unum necessarium*, c. 18; cf. my work *Comenius* (1982).

48

for the reforming and more humane renewing of secular and ecclesiastical relations in school, church, and society. Here again, however, there can be no talk of an overhasty equating of the kingdom of God with human orders. The labyrinth of the world remains a labyrinth. But within this labyrinth the hope of the kingdom is to be kept alive in persistent humanitarian advances and projects. Here again it is true that those who wander in the direction of the kingdom and pray for its coming will try, in prayer and action, to love earth and God in one.

The Future of Him Who Has Come

Let us now try to clarify the content of the second petition. What does it say theologically in its New Testament sense? I will begin with the first word of the Greek text: *eltheto*, "may it come." Already in antiquity the word was used for what was often coming in a theological sense, especially in cultic prayers as a request for divine *parousia*, for the god to come and save. We see this in the prayer of Odysseus in Homer: "Hear me, goddess, come graciously to help me" (*Iliad* 23.770). Of New Testament usage, too, it can be said that "the word belongs to the circle of ideas connected with the divine epiphany."[7] This is definitely so when the New Testament is referring to the coming of the Son of Man or the coming of the kingdom of God. At issue here is the eschatological salvation-event, the final turn in the times in both a personal and a cosmic sense. "*Basileia theou, ho aion ho archomenos* and *zoe aionios* are different expressions for the one actuality of salvation."[8] This includes the future but already impinges on the present. It is to this tension-laden horizon that the unassuming word "come" directs the petition.

From it we learn something essential about the New Testament understanding of time. We must always remember that in

7. J. Schneider, *TDNT*, 2:668.
8. Ibid., p. 670.

the book of Revelation the reality of God spans time and eternity: He is and was and is to come (1:4, 8; 4:8). In enumerating the three dimensions, we should note that the verse does not say about the future: He will be, but: He is to come. Time is understood in terms of the eschatological coming of the kingdom. This is the determinative view in the Old Testament as well. Time is not a mechanical or linear series of banal units. It is qualified, directed to a goal, and both potentially and actually meaningful. It is not *chronos*, a mechanically measurable concept, but *kairos*, the opportune hour, to which we must react, not neutrally as waiting spectators, but with involvement, making a decision either for or against. This gives time its unique significance and even tension. As Lohmeyer said, "There is no infinite flow of becoming which streams incessantly onwards, but only a coming and a becoming, new like the sun every morning, until through God's counsel this becoming reaches its true destiny and arrives at the end of all coming."[9] Hence we can and should make the most of the time (cf. Eph. 5:16; Col. 4:5), not letting it pass by idly, but grasping it and filling it with prayer and action. When time is seen in this way, to pass it or sleep it away unthinkingly and in limitless distraction is to set life at risk and to lose it (cf. the parable of the ten virgins, Matt. 25:1-13). Cultivated boredom is in this sense a mortal sin.

The time defined by the eschatological "may it come" is marked by another emphasis. Our time, especially our future, is personalized. Some European languages hint at this aspect, for example, French *avenir* or German *Zukunft*, which in distinction from *futurum* view future time as *adveniens*, as coming to us. This personalizing of time is even more concrete in the specific Christian sense. Our future carries the historical and eschatological characteristics of the person of Jesus of Nazareth. He is the one who comes to us. What comes is finally he who comes. This at least is the New Testament view. Its final position is unmistakable. From the Synoptics, with their message of the *parousia* of the Son of Man in salvation and judgment, to Revelation, he who

9. Lohmeyer, *"Lord's Prayer,"* p. 95.

is to come is the Lord who is manifest in Jesus. The last prayer, a clear and noteworthy appendix to our petition, is as follows: "Amen. Come, Lord Jesus" (Rev. 22:20).

For me the work of the ecumenical community has unforgettably expressed and confirmed this aspect, especially the World Assembly at Evanston in 1954, which in its preparatory document gave to those who were asking what would become of the world the reply "His kingdom is coming," and to those who asked what is ahead of us, the reply that we do not stand facing a trackless waste of unfulfilled time with a goal that no one can venture to predict, but look to our living Lord, our Judge and Savior, who was dead and who ever lives, to the one who came and comes and will for ever reign, so that although we may run into troubles, and will do so if we want to have a part in him, we know his word, his royal word: "Be of good cheer, I have overcome the world."

The inner closeness and indeed identity of the subjects of the two basic forms of the New Testament petition "come"—the kingdom of God and the Lord Jesus—are of vital importance if we are to achieve a more precise understanding of God's kingdom. How often in church history and world history this central thought of Jesus has been viewed as a general idea! The motif has played an important part in theology and church history and is also present in the history of Western philosophy and culture. One has only to consult the seven volumes of Ernst Staehelin's work *Die Verkündigung des Reiches Gottes in der Kirche Jesu Christi* to realize how many variations there have been in understanding the concept. I might mention Hobbes and Locke, Lessing and Kant, Herder and Hegel, and many others. Measured by the original biblical use many such attempts have been very free and even arbitrary. We often have the impression that the idea of the kingdom of God is treated as an empty vessel that may be filled according to individual priorities.

Theology need not immediately make a vigorous protest against this use or misuse of the message of God's kingdom. The variety is a sign that the kingdom is not a monopoly of the church but jumps across its boundaries. This accords, as we have seen, with the original thrust of the motif. Even in unusual ways many humanitarian initiatives have been launched under its banner. Yet it is still the task of theology to draw attention insistently to the New Testament content of the kingdom. In the Bible the idea is not vague or Proteus-like; it has unmistakable contours. It is embodied and outlined in the history of Jesus of Nazareth. Origen correctly grasped this when he defined the kingdom as the *autobasileia* of Jesus Christ. The great heretic of the early church, Marcion, was also right on this point when, as quoted by Tertullian, he summed up the same insight in the brief statement that "in the gospel the kingdom of God is Christ himself." We have to look in this direction if we want to understand the second petition in biblical terms. The message, practice, and destiny of Jesus are of normative significance in this regard.

At its heart the message of Jesus is the good news of the coming kingdom of God, of its liberating promise and claim. As K. L. Schmidt said, the gospel is that of the kingdom of God.[10] We need think only of the parables—almost all of them concern the mystery of the kingdom. Or especially the Sermon on the Mount: What is it but the constitution and intimation of the kingdom? An even more important point: The deeds as well as the words of Jesus present the kingdom. I think of the healings, which are viewed as signs of the kingdom not only by those outside but by Jesus himself: "If it is by the finger of God that I cast out demons, then the kingdom of God has come upon you" (Luke 11:20). Even further and more profoundly, the rule of God may be seen not only in his acts but in his Easter destiny, his cross and resurrection. This is clearly how the New Testament sees it. On the way of the Man of Nazareth from the crib to the cross and the empty tomb, the kingdom of God has drawn near. "Jesus comes in and with His kingdom."[11] As Calvin rightly put it: "When Christ could be pointed out with the finger, the Kingdom of God was opened."[12]

---

10. K. L. Schmidt, *TDNT*, 1:583.
11. Schneider, *TDNT*, 2:670.
12. Calvin, *Institutes*, 1:455, § 2.11.5.

The Kingdom for Today and Tomorrow

Let us try to grasp more closely the concept and reality of the kingdom of God as Jesus viewed it. But first we must be warned not to try to arrive at a definition or clear-cut systematization. This is not possible. The words and person of Jesus resist it. We have to remember that Jesus liked to speak of the kingdom in parables, that is, in a form of speech which is consciously provisional, which conceals as well as reveals the mystery of the kingdom (Mark 4:11). We can never lay hold of this mystery or conceptualize it. We can only give hints of it in the form of a sketch.

In the New Testament witness to God's kingdom two lines come together which at a first glance seem to be heterogeneous. The first presents the *basileia tou theou* in some sense spatially—in analogy, though in definite contrast, to earthly kingdoms. Typical phrases point in this direction. We can enter the kingdom (Matt. 5:20; 7:21; 18:3; etc.). We can be put out of it (8:12). There are keys to it (16:19). It can be closed by men (23:13). The images of a house and a city are evoked. In the parables these can be very concrete, for example, the father's house, or a king's house to which one can be invited and in which one can be regarded and treated as a member of the household. The disciples are described as sons of the kingdom (8:12) or as invited guests (22:3, 8-9). They are promised special fellowship with the king or the father. They may sit at table (8:11), eat and drink (Luke 22:30), and take part in a marriage feast (Matt. 22:1-14; 25:1-13).

But this house and kingdom in the message of Jesus are not an exclusive residence for the privileged. The fellowship is not a closed fellowship. The doors of this city are wide open. In distinction from some tendencies in Judaism (e.g., the Qumran community), Jesus stressed the breaking down of solid barriers between the people of Israel and other peoples, often in sharp polemic against those who are born into the inheritance, the sons of the kingdom. Taking up the eschatological message of the prophets, in an encounter with one who came in out of the cold, he told his listeners: "I tell you, many will come from east and

west and sit at table with Abraham, Isaac, and Jacob in the kingdom of heaven, while the sons of the kingdom will be thrown
into the outer darkness" (Matt. 8:11-12). The kingdom of God is
not under the control of hereditary administrators. Jesus turns
to the rejected, to those that suffer discrimination. His call goes
out to the weary and heavy laden (11:28). His table fellowship
is with sinners (9:10; Luke 5:29). This is the tendency, indeed, the
basic constitution, of the kingdom.

This understanding or trend in the message of Jesus is to
a large extent new. In the Old Testament the kingdom occurs in
this sense only on the margin. But there is a second trend or line,
and in this regard the Old Testament witness is strong. One can
view the *basileia tou theou* as rule or royal dominion. This understanding is deeply and centrally anchored in the Old Testament,
whose witnesses know and praise Yahweh as the true King of
Israel: "The Lord [literally, Yahweh] will reign [or is King] for
ever and ever" (Exod. 15:18). This confession retained its validity even when Israel wanted an earthly king after the manner of
the Gentiles. Israel did so with hesitation and obvious disquiet,
because with good reason they feared that in the monarchy there
would be apostasy from the true kingship of God (1 Sam. 8). Yet
precisely in times of decline the prophets kept alive recollection
of the true King. Indeed, not just the memory but the hope of
God's kingdom was kept alive in the Old Testament.

This memory and hope had liberating results. The reminder that God reigns helped to demythologize the human
world, including political authority. No king, kingdom, or power
on earth can set itself on the supreme throne. No one on earth
may claim absolute obedience. God reigns. Furthermore, hope of
the royal rule of Yahweh breaks open the present, closed though
it may seem, freely to the future, showing that our place in history is not one of fate but of destiny, the place of our testing.

In this regard we should not overlook that with increasing
clarity the hope and recollection are eschatologically grounded
and oriented. This means first that they relate to the promises
and faithfulness of God, not to the powers and processes of history. It is a matter of his lordship, not of our kingdoms. Again,

the horizon of hope is derestricted eschatologically. Although the coming kingdom can be lauded as the coming kingdom of our father David (cf. Mark 11:10), it is the kingdom which in judgment and salvation is the future not merely of Israel but of all peoples. For the King of Israel is not a local god; he is the Creator of heaven and earth.

The prophetic message of the liberating reign of God is fully adopted by Jesus in his words and deeds. We cannot understand his way apart from the related eschatological disposition. He teaches and heals on the presupposition that the last and decisive hour has already come: "The kingdom of God is at hand" (Mark 1:15). In the prism of their Easter experience, the New Testament witnesses confirm the presupposition with varied but unanimous voices. In the person and history of Jesus of Nazareth the lordship of God has become flesh once for all and definitively. In him the kingdom of God was and is among us (Luke 17:21).

The two circles of ideas that are bound up with the thought of God's kingdom in the New Testament—the vividly concrete, spatial, everyday view on the one side, the confession of God's kingly rule that is oriented to the final future on the other—stake out the field of tension for the petition "Thy kingdom come." The tension of the two lines is constitutive for the New Testament understanding of the world, and it distinguishes this view from the other eschatological and apocalyptic ideas of the day. As Lohmeyer says, it "has stripped the idea of the 'coming world' of the characteristics of apocalyptic fantasy and mystical indeterminacy and has given it the imminent reality of an historical event; it has removed the kingdom of God from its previously historical context and enlarged it so that it becomes the 'coming world' of God, to which 'many come from the east and from the west.'... That is the significance of this unity, that God's apocalyptically unique and eternal reality and his historically unique activity are regarded as an event which happens here and now and in the future."[13] The implications of this view for

13. Lohmeyer, *"Lord's Prayer,"* 99-100.

our understanding of the world we shall have to consider later. Provisionally, however, we may say that against this background the petition "Thy kingdom come" is neither a flight from the concrete conditions of our world nor a capitulation to them.

A note concerning the understanding of biblical eschatology seems to be in order in this connection. This eschatology stands or falls, especially in the New Testament, with the motif of the kingdom of God. The tension already mentioned finds a parallel in the timing. In some texts the kingdom of God is plainly a future event. As in apocalyptic modes of thought, its coming is expected at the end of the days. But there are also emphatic passages, especially in relation to the work of Jesus, which speak of the gradual growth of the kingdom (the parable of the grain of mustard seed, Matt. 13:31-32, that of the leaven, v. 33). Then there are those which depict its coming as a future, cosmic catastrophe (the Synoptic Apocalypse, Mark 13 par.). It is no wonder that New Testament scholars are divided about future or realized eschatology, depending on which view they stress as normative.

In contrast, my Prague teacher J. B. Souček, trying to overcome false alternatives, coined the formula "double eschatology." Biblically he was right, though I myself would prefer to speak of a double view. The apostolic witnesses and confessors in the primitive church looked both ways, to him that had come and to him that is to come, yet they had no doubt as to the identity of him to whom they looked. It was Jesus Christ, "the same yesterday and today and for ever" (Heb. 13:8). Our future is the future of him who has come (W. Kreck). His kingdom is not just the power at the end of our lives but in the middle of them. "Thy kingdom come" has to do with our today as well as our tomorrow.

The First Step of Conversion

In what way does it have to do with our today? What does the petition mean for our understanding of the world and the shaping of our lives? What are its implications? We shall go into these questions in this final part of our exposition. In so doing I will start at the key saying of Jesus: "The kingdom of God is at hand; repent, and believe in the gospel" (Mark 1:15). The imperative of the second half of this saying corresponds to the indicative of the first. The normative terms are repentance (better: conversion) and faith. These terms imply two motifs.

It is worth noting that conversion comes first in any relevant response to God's coming kingdom. This is by no means self-evident. We have noted already that in the history of the exposition of God's kingdom the idea was only too easily construed in terms of a prolongation of human ideals, the climax of human aspirations. The New Testament takes a different view. The kingdom is not the climax of our ideals or our good will but cuts right across these. It means conversion. To be sure, the kingdom of God is more than a polemical concept. Yet it has a delimiting, polemical side. Augustine was not wrong when he contrasted the city of God with the city of the devil. There is such a contrast, even though we may not agree with the philosophy of history that is worked out in terms of it. It is sobering, but is also in the interests of a biblically responsible understanding, to maintain that the second petition of the Lord's Prayer swims against the current of our own history to the extent that this is the history of our interests, or, as Marx would say, the history of class conflicts, as it very largely is. In making this petition we truly stand in opposition to ourselves, to the wishes and tendencies of our own hearts.

Rudolf Bohren brings out the polemical sharpness of the petition in connection with everyday situations. He asks whether we know what we are praying for when we pray "Thy kingdom come." We are praying first that our own kingdoms may perish, our human kingdoms. The kingdom of businessmen bending over filing cabinets, of housewives lovingly looking at their crockery, of workers going to their lathes, of hospital patients opening their sidetable drawers. We all have our kingdoms, large or small. We all have our spheres of life in which we reign. There are many such kingdoms. Hence many of us pray "Thy kingdom come" with our lips, but with our hearts we pray "No, no, my kingdom come."[14]

One might object that this is all very trifling, given color by various banal examples. These are not battles for the kingdom of God; at most they are only skirmishes in everyday life. One might almost refer to Ephesians: "For we are not contending against flesh and blood, but against the principalities, against the powers, against the world rulers of this present darkness, against the spiritual hosts of wickedness in the heavenly places" (6:12). Nevertheless, we have to consider that in the Gospels human decisions regarding the kingdom of God are often bound up with small but very painful decisions in everyday life. I have in mind the radically sharp words of Jesus to potential followers. If, as we can easily understand, someone answers the call to discipleship with the request "I will follow you, Lord, but let me first say farewell to those at home," Jesus replies: "No one who puts his hand to the plow and looks back is fit for the kingdom of God" (Luke 9:61-62). Deliberate and resolute conversion is needed.

In some hours and situations even and especially today the call for resolute conversion can have unheard-of force and come monstrously close to reality. I am writing these sentences a few months after the Chernobyl disaster and some weeks after the night in Basel (Nov. 1, 1986) which posed such a threat to life. These events truly shook us up in Basel. We could not overlook the fact that the call for conversion again went forth in persistent and palpably concerned reaction to these events. Sometimes the call might be too emotional and barely adequate, yet we can understand it and respect it, and basically it was right. We should welcome it that in this context the churches remembered their inheritance, which includes the motif of conversion and its clear enunciation in the light of God's kingdom.

I recall the statement of the Basel Synod of November 26, 1986. We have been reminded afresh, it says, "that the liberating power of the gospel comes out in our readiness for conver-

14. Bohren, *Das Unser Vater—heute* (Zurich: 1960), p. 41.

sion. We confess that in the goals of our political and personal action we have often been too one-sidedly oriented to economic interests without sufficiently taking into account our fellows in other lands and our fellow creatures in the environment. What is due is life-promoting conversion in the sense of the gospel. We want to support in our congregations and city a life-style of solidarity which will be more peaceful and kinder to the environment." Unquestionably, those who take seriously the signs of the times will have to ponder and practice biblical *metanoia* with a new intensity.

In one respect these considerations are more to the point than the examples given by Bohren. The main attack of God's kingdom is not on symptoms but on the root of all evil, radical evil in our human world. In this regard we must take very seriously what Ephesians says about principalities and powers. In the last chapter of his exposition of the Lord's Prayer, which dealt with this petition, Karl Barth rightly gave much attention to this problem. He speaks there of the "lordless powers" which the petition has primarily in view. What does he mean by this?

The root of all evil is the disruption of the cosmic order by our human falling away from the Creator. The tragic results of the Fall have a paradoxical aspect: "Parallel to the history of his [man's] emancipation from God there runs that of the emancipation of his own possibilities of life from himself: the history of the overpowering of his desires, aspirations, and will by the power, the superpower, of his ability."[15] Like Goethe's sorcerer's apprentice, he becomes the victim of the lordless powers that he has conjured up but can no longer control, which have come to lord it over him. We are movers, but we are also moved. It is only mythically that we can speak of this fact, of our entanglement in the world of evil, and the Bible speaks of it in the terms that we find in Ephesians 6.

Yet even today, and perhaps precisely today, we can verify and illustrate the sober reality behind the mythical language. Barth himself gives a series of examples. He refers to the myth

15. Barth, *Christian Life,* p. 214.

59

of the state, to the absolutizing of its power, which makes of an instrument of human order the apparatus of blind government and oppression. He thinks of the destructive power of mammon, the rule and sway of the profit motive, to which countless people, especially at the bottom but also at the top of the social ladder, fall victim. He also mentions the perverting rule of ideology, which so often tries to put those who fashion it on the Procrustean bed of its dictates and in this way to deform them. He critically surveys the chthonic powers, which include technology, at first a liberating and then a threatening and controlling force, which, as we now see more clearly, is increasingly destroying the environment. They also include less harmful powers such as sport and fashion.

The strategy or model of alienation is always the same. In our fall from the Creator the powers and potentialities that are innate in creation and humanity become false absolutes in relation to us. This strategy of alienation has brought us to the very edge of the final threat, the piling up in what seems to be a fatally necessary way of weapons of unimaginable destructive power. This is a development which might be added today to Barth's analysis as its critical climax.

Against this dark background and into this dark abyss moves the petition for the coming of God's kingdom. In it is the first step of conversion and in this sense it is the one thing necessary. If our fall from the Creator is the beginning of disaster, the approach to him in petition and intercession is the beginning of healing. As Barth said in connection with the Lord's Prayer and this petition, folding our hands in prayer is the beginning of revolt against the disorder of the world. It is the beginning, not the end. A sober and objective analysis of the mechanisms of alienation (such as Marx gave of an economy dominated by the profit motive) and a practical political initiative in the search for alternatives must then follow. For Christians, however, praying for the kingdom of God is where the turn is made. It is the first step of conversion.

The State of the World Will Be Renewed

The petition "Thy kingdom come" is a call for faith as well as for conversion: "And believe in the gospel." The kingdom of God is more than a critical authority, more than a warning light at the entry to our personal and social dead ends. The message of the kingdom certainly includes awareness of judgment, of the seriousness of human decision. But it is gospel, good news, oriented to hope. God's kingdom is by nature light, Advent light, *adveniat regnum tuum*. It is word of promise and reality of promise, an invitation to faith, to life in the perspective of promise.

What does this mean for our understanding of the world and the shaping of our lives? We find an answer in the story of the first sermon of Jesus in Luke 4:14-21. Already this text is important for our theme because it is the Lucan parallel to Mark's summary of the initial ministry of Jesus, which Luke, too, describes as proclamation of the kingdom of God (4:43). The heart of the sermon is this: "The Spirit of the Lord is upon me, because he has anointed me to preach good news to the poor. He has sent me to proclaim release to the captives and recovering of sight to the blind, to set at liberty those who are oppressed, to proclaim the acceptable year of the Lord."

This is a quotation from Isaiah 61:1-2, the basic word of hope for Israel, the promise of the liberating and reconciling future of God. Jesus preaches on this text. His sermon is summed up in the brief statement: "Today this scripture has been fulfilled in your hearing." A short sermon, yet one that contains the whole program of God's kingdom. What Isaiah promised for the last, messianic future of God, Jesus says is already present. The promise of reconciliation and liberation is not a song about some utopian future remote from reality. The promises break into our relations and conditions.

A new relation to reality is pioneered. It is not a fanatical one. It takes relations seriously. A striking feature is how many pressures and threats in the human world it considers. Isaiah and Jesus do not flee to heavenly heights. They point to the depths of the very real relations that oppress us all. They mention suffering people, groups and individuals. There are the poor, the failures, both in the economic sense—the hungry and unemployed—and also in the moral and religious sense—the despised and ignored whom the official church and society suspect and exclude. Then there are prisoners, oppressed people who have made mistakes, who are dependent on the favor of the privileged and rulers, servants and slaves who have no freedom or human rights. There are also the blind, the physically and mentally handicapped, the sick, with their reduced potentialities. There are also the defeated, those who have suffered shipwreck through outer blows or inner failure and collapse. They are all there, the whole human race, all of us with our own special needs. Unquestionably, Jesus does not ignore the relations and pressures of the day but mentions them individually: poverty, injustice, sickness, and oppression.

Yet in the light of the kingdom of God this ungilded view of things is not the whole reality. The human race, all of us with our needs, we are not alone, we are not left to our own devices, we are not given up to the superior power of relations. Instead we are set in the perspective of the promise. Adopting the message of the prophets, Jesus speaks good news to the poor, freedom to the captives, sight to the blind, and deliverance to the oppressed. Human need is comprehensive and many-faceted. But even more comprehensive and many-faceted is the promise of God.

Being a disciple of the kingdom of God means constantly trying to confront situations with promises and promises with situations. This is an urgent and relevant task today. The horizons of our modern world are dark. If we look only at situations, at the state of the world as it is, an honest balance sheet would be alarming and depressing. We must agree with the verdict of Erich Fried that those who want the world to remain as it is do not want it to remain at all (Status quo *zur Zeit des Wettrüstens*).

Yet precisely at this point we can and should pray "Thy kingdom come." This is a Nevertheless prayer. It does not wipe out the problems mentioned but sets them in the context of the kingdom of God. In this way it relativizes them, robbing them of their final validity. *Kyrios Christos:* The Risen Lord is the Lord of principalities and powers. This liberates us. We are no longer the prisoners of omnipotent fate. As in the days of the apostles, so today belief in the kingdom of God proves to be a resistance movement against fatalism. Our world must not remain as it is. Resistance is possible; our hearts and circumstances can change. The principalities and powers, sinful entanglements and destructive structures, do not have us fully in their grip. We must steadfastly remove them and direct our steps to the coming kingdom of God. The young Karl Barth stated this impressively if with some exaggeration in the first edition of his commentary on Romans: "The kingdom of God is a kingdom of the liberated and the free; it is a kingdom of kings, and our human will may be active with a view to this kingdom, it may accept what grace offers it as a free gift. God's grace sets us in motion once again towards immediacy and freedom. . . . There is to be no more arrogance or hubris when we believe in our liberation from evil and wrestle and fight for the fulfilment of our glorious destiny."[16]

It makes a decisive difference to culture and society if there are groups within them that amid the oppressions of time keep their eyes open to the kingdom of God, praying for it and following it in the direction that Christ's promises indicate, that is, by taking up the cause of the poor, acting on behalf of prisoners and the handicapped, freeing the oppressed, and especially proclaiming the acceptable year of the Lord, the liberating future of God. The state of the world will be renewed.

The state of the *world* will be renewed. How are we to understand this? First, of course, in line with the promises quoted from Luke 4. The hope of the kingdom relates primarily to the renewal of human hearts and circumstances, to human history and society, to the new city as it appears in a way that all can see at the end of the New Testament, in Revelation 21. Yet in its final scope the hope of the kingdom goes further and embraces the

---

16. Barth, *Der Römerbrief,* 1st ed. (Bern: 1919; repr. Zurich: 1963), pp. 141-42.

new heaven and the new earth. Bonhoeffer was right when, expounding the petition, he fully stressed not only "God and humanity" but also "God and the world," and when even more pointedly he brought together "God and the earth." In the context of the kingdom of God we finally see the eschatological outline of the new creation. The promise is not only for us and for our history; it is finally also for our fellow creatures, for all nature.

It may seem bold to stretch the line of the petition that far. Yet there are good biblical reasons to do so. In the Old Testament the prophetic vision, as we see very clearly in Isaiah 11, embraces not only human kingdoms but also the animal kingdom in its hope for an eschatological reign of peace. In the New Testament we have referred already to Romans 8, which against an eschatological background impressively and emphatically stresses the solidarity of the children of God with the creation that is implicated in their history of guilt (Rom. 8:19ff.).

In the light of the increasingly visible results of our graceless dealing with creation, I can see today why some of the eighteenth-century theologians who were most faithful to the Bible (e.g., F. C. Oetinger, the devout philanthropist Johann Caspar Lavater, or the evangelist John Wesley) emphatically related their hope of the kingdom of God to the inner and outer material and natural world, to the world around us, and did so with an accent on renewal. Thus Wesley, in expounding this petition, spoke of the participation of all rational creatures in the renewal of all things, and in a sermon on Romans 8 he went even further and spoke of a universal liberation in virtue of which all animals would be "restored, not only to the vigor, strength and swiftness which they had at their first creation, but to a far higher degree."[17] The kingdom of God encourages solidarity not only with our fellows, to whom it gives priority, but also with all our fellow creatures.

17. John Wesley, *Works* (London: 1872), 6:249.

Righteousness, Peace, and Joy

We conclude with a reference to Paul. We have hardly mentioned him in expounding the second petition. This is understandable, for whereas the kingdom of God is incontestably at the heart of the message in the Synoptic Gospels, it occurs only on the margin in Paul. Yet almost incidentally the apostle offers a statement which pregnantly sums up the main emphasis of the biblical message of the kingdom. I have in mind Romans 14:17, where he says: "The kingdom of God is righteousness and peace and joy in the Holy Spirit." Is not this triad a very precise summary of the biblical message of the kingdom?

Righteousness: Jesus himself made it very clear that the prayer for the kingdom of God is as it were in one breath linked to the prayer for righteousness and the doing of righteousness before God and among our fellows: "But seek first his kingdom and his righteousness, and all these things shall be yours as well" (Matt. 6:33). *Peace,* Old Testament *shalom:* This is the quintessence of definitive salvation and therefore of the kingdom of God as the Old Testament prophets proclaimed it and the New Testament witnesses understood it. The testimony is that the whole history of Jesus, from the Christmas greeting of the angels to the Easter greeting of the Risen Lord, is God's initiative of peace. *Joy in the Holy Spirit:* How can we miss this in the message of Jesus? The kingdom of God in the Gospels is the epitome of joy: wedding, banquet, harvest; feasting, rejoicing, dancing.[18]

The threefold note of righteousness, peace, and joy is the leading one in the polyphony of the kingdom of God. It should stamp all our praying and doing from the standpoint of God's kingdom. We should not isolate one or the other voice, nor arbitrarily accord prominence to one or the other motif, but give due emphasis to all of them in mutual relationship *(perichoresis).* Joy without righteousness, we might say, would not be peace-

---

18. Cf. H.-J. Kraus, *Reich Gottes—Reich der Freiheit* (Neukirchen-Vluyn: Neukirchener, 1975), p. 22.

ful, and peace without righteousness would be indolent. But righteousness and peace without joy would fall far short.

I want to stress the importance of this third little sister that is often underrated, joy in the Holy Spirit. How often the best-intentioned efforts for righteousness and peace are tainted and unconvincing because in their glum moroseness the life-giving element of joy is missing. "The kingdom of God is . . . joy in the Holy Spirit." "Great joy will come to all people" (Luke 2:10); these words of the angel at the beginning of the life of Jesus are unmistakable. They speak of joy even before they speak of righteousness and peace. We should never forget this.

In his exposition of the petition, Bonhoeffer rightly says that the hour at which the church today prays for the kingdom of God forces it for better or for worse into fellowship with the children of the earth and the world and pledges it to faithfulness to the earth even to hunger and to death.[19] We must take this seriously. Yet we must add, and we think Bonhoeffer would agree, that the hour at which the church today prays for the kingdom of God is and always will be, in spite of the dark horizon, the hour of great joy. For we do not pray in the void or the dark. We pray on the way to the coming kingdom. Righteousness, peace, and joy are not chimeras. They are promises of the kingdom which God fulfilled and guaranteed in Jesus. We go toward them in our pilgrimage. In spite of everything, the future is theirs. With anxiety then, yet also with confidence, we pray: "Thy kingdom come."

---

19. Bonhoeffer, *Gesammelte Schriften,* 3:274.

Thy Will Be Done,
on Earth as It Is in Heaven

Resistance and Submission

The petition that God's will should be done, and that we should bring our own will and conduct into conformity with it, is part of the patrimony of the piety of antiquity. The following story is told about the Pythagorean philosopher Thymaridas. When he parted from his friends to go on a sea voyage, the wish was expressed that the gods would do for him whatever he wanted. But he replied: "God forbid, may I want whatever the gods do for me." The devout are not content with the only too human wish that the gods will prove well-disposed to them. They strive higher than that, wanting to show that they are people who will steadfastly say yes to the rule and sway of the gods. Not my will but thine be done.

This attitude is particularly well documented in the case of popular Hellenistic philosophy of a Stoic cast. Epictetus, who recommended surrender to the divine will in many different ways, quotes the poet Cleanthes: "Lead me, O Zeus, O mighty fate, wherever I am commanded to go according to your counsel; if I, a transgressor, should refuse to follow, I would still be made to follow" (*Enchiridion* 53).

We must not overlook the worldview that lies behind this piety. It was stamped by the spirit of religious determinism. The world supposedly lies under an inescapable law. Whether it be viewed as divine omnipotence, the power of fate, or the self-enclosed necessity of natural processes—and all such definitions are possible from this standpoint—the result is the same, namely, that our destiny is interwoven into the cosmic whole and that there is no possibility of breaking out of the predetermined circle of determinative forces or of autonomously altering the course of things. Our only sensible possibility is to become aware of the basic conditioning of existence and to adjust to it willingly and without defiance. The willing are led by fate, the unwilling are dragged by it (*volentem fata ducunt, nolentem trahunt*). So runs an old Stoic proverb. A dramatic illustration from Epictetus depicts the human situation. It is like that of a dog that is harnessed to a cart and has to go downhill. It can feel free only so long as it runs ahead of the cart, but if it tries to slow down or to stop, it is run over. Since we can do nothing to resist divine fate, we do well to fit in with it. Our only chance lies in acts of prudent submission to the gods, to fate, or to cosmic processes. Submission is the supreme virtue and the only freedom of religious people. "Thy will be done" is the basic prayer.

In the history of the exposition and impact of Jesus' petition "Thy will be done," there have undoubtedly been tendencies that remind us of this piety of antiquity. We all know devout hymns and devotional writings which take and apply the words of the petition along these lines. I might refer to hymns by Paul Gerhardt (1653), Georg Neumark (1657), and Karl Rudolf Hagenbach (1846) in which they accept God's way and quietly submit to his rule.

We can understand the reference of such hymns. In some situations in human life we are apparently or genuinely confronted by what is irrevocable and unalterable. We see this in the social sphere. How many people lose for decades all chances of a meaningful life through political or economic upheavals! We also see it even more frequently in the personal sphere. Fate deals us many blows: sickness and death, collapse of plans, failure and betrayal. In such situations the most natural reaction is defiance. But is it the wisest? Might it not be more prudent to accept the hard blows of fate for what they might be, namely, the instruments of a decree which is certainly bitter, terrifying, and hard to understand, but still divine? In this way might there not come even in the darkest hours some measure of light, a partial liberation? At times life is indeed like the running of the dog in the ancient illustration. It then makes a difference whether we let ourselves be led or have to be dragged by the events and processes of history either great or small. It makes a difference whether we beat our heads against the wall or say once again, perhaps gritting our teeth: "Thy will be done."

It has impressed me strongly that in some situations the people of the Bible do adopt this attitude. I have in mind Jeremiah and his attempt to master the unhappy political situation of his people by faith in God's disposing and overruling. The trial was hard and things even seemed hopeless. All the people's political hopes had been frustrated. Enslavement for generations was the sobering and frightening prospect. To defy seemed to be the only option, though this, too, was hopeless. Yet in this dark social and personal situation the man of sorrows, severely tempted and tested, called for submission to the will of God and for the renunciation of autonomous dreams and plans with all that they might entail politically. Even in exile the good of the city (Jer. 29:7), the good of an alien city, must be sought. This was a demand without parallel, yet it was better than persistent defiance. It offered a small chance of regaining the lost freedom. If the people could accept the blows and disasters not as blind fate but as possibly and actually the judgment of God, hard though it might be to grasp and understand, then, possibly against the grain and only very soberly and modestly, a new beginning could be made. "Thy will be done" would then in fact be the sign and signal of a new beginning.

The intellectual basis of this prophetic submissiveness was very different, of course, from that of the piety of antiquity. We have seen that the presupposition of the religiophilosophical attitude was awareness that cosmic things are predetermined and ineluctable. The mood was one of religious fatalism corresponding to the Stoic and Hellenistic worldview. Nor to this alone! Even more strongly we find fatalistic streams of thought in religious history: passively in the Indian religions with their idea of *samsara*, of the inescapably foreordained cycles of rebirth; actively in Islam, in which the will of God rules immutably and fixes every step that we take as *kismet*, so that everything we do, even to the point of suicide missions, can be equated with the will of Allah.

The biblical view of the cosmos, and especially of human history, differs widely from fatalism of that type. We are not caught in the net of unchangeable cosmic forces and laws. God created the world. Creation is open to the future. Human life is not the running of a dog. It is a dynamic affair, full of reverses, often hard to understand, often impenetrable, yet never without options and situations of decision, however limited, in the tension between perdition and salvation. On the biblical view God is not an anonymous destiny. He is not the force of events that are in some way inevitable. He is not a hard necessity to which we must adjust. It is essential that we recall at this point the invocation of the Lord's Prayer. God is our Father in heaven, the God in covenant with us, the more than necessary one, the God of his liberating name. His will is not an iron will. It is a living will with the vitality of love. It is not already fixed once and for all. God is not an abstract principle after the model of "let justice be done even though the world perish." His will is capable of dialog, of rethinking, of repentance in the sense of free reactions to the differing responses of his creatures. It aims at their salvation, liberation, and reconciliation. "Who is a God like thee, pardoning iniquity and passing over transgression for the remnant of his inheritance? He does not retain his anger for ever because he delights in steadfast love" (Mic. 7:18). This will can even be "crossed," not by the arrogance of the unfaithful, but by the prayer of the poor. "The prayer of a righteous man has great power in its effects" (Jas. 5:16).

This means that if we pray "Thy will be done" to a God of this kind, our prayer is not to be confused with prudent resig-

70

nation or pious capitulation, with the desire not to be out of the predetermined cycle but always and everywhere to be in step with the gods. It is more a matter of the cry of those who pray to God that he would establish his declared will—his kingdom—among us. Seen in this way, the petition does not drug the devout. It does not make them ready to accept without question anything that might come. It is not a spiritual anesthetic or opiate to reconcile them a priori to circumstances. On the contrary, it encourages them constantly to orient themselves to the true will of God, which means, as we recall from our discussion of the previous petition, to confront circumstances with promises. For not everything that happens is unquestionably in accordance with God's will. Much of an alien will may be seen in the creation of the free God. The powers of darkness have made themselves mighty in every way and brought forth unmentionably more corruption than one can name in every age.[1] Precisely at this point we have to test the spirits, confronting circumstances with promises, with the revealed will of God.

With the word "submission" I have indicated the most obvious response to the third petition of the Lord's Prayer. I am not withdrawing it. But in the light of what has just been said I must supplement it. The petition "Thy will be done" demands resistance as well as submission. Eberhard Bethge used these two terms as the German title (*Widerstand und Ergebung*) when editing Bonhoeffer's letters and papers from prison. They make a good title, bringing out the essential motif of the fragments. The tragic disruption of Bonhoeffer's life, his bound hands in a Nazi prison, the interrupted personal and theological plans which so concerned him—these gave to the theme of meaningful submission a special force. Yet even in prison Bonhoeffer was a resistance fighter. He looked back on his decision to fight Hitler, which he had made resolutely, but not easily. For him, therefore, the question of the relation between submission and resistance, or perhaps one might say between passive and active obedience, was an urgent one.

1. See J. C. Blumhardt, *Das Vaterunser*, 4th ed. (Basel: 1946), pp. 34-35.

Bonhoeffer dealt with the theme not merely in occasional references in other connections but also in a direct discussion of the tension-laden problem. His answer is worth noting if we want to understand the reference of the prayer in its biblical richness.

> I've often wondered here where we are to draw the line between necessary resistance to "fate," and equally necessary submission. Don Quixote is the symbol of resistance carried to the point of absurdity, even lunacy; and similarly, Michael Kohlhaas, insisting on his rights, puts himself in the wrong . . . in both cases resistance at last defeats its own object, and evaporates in theoretical fantasy. Sancho Panza is the type of complacent and artful accommodation to things as they are. . . . We must confront fate—to me the neuter gender of the word "fate" (*Schicksal*) is significant—as resolutely as we submit to it at the right time . . . . It's therefore impossible to define the boundary between resistance and submission on abstract principles; but both of them must exist, and both must be practiced.[2]

The Saving Dynamic of God's Will

It is time to focus more sharply on the biblical meaning of the term "will," and especially of God's will. Let me begin with a basic observation. In general philosophical usage we think of the will as the organ or act of willing that is proper to a subject, human or divine. In church history the term occurs in many contexts in this sense. I might refer to the Monothelite controversy in the early church. The issue then was whether Jesus Christ, the God-Man, has only the one divine will or two wills, the divine will and the human. A very different context was that of the medieval debate between voluntarists and rationalists. Either in us or in God, does reason or will take precedence? Again, how passionately at the time of the Reformation was the issue of the

2. Bonhoeffer, *Letters and Papers from Prison*, pp. 217-18.

free or enslaved will debated between Erasmus and Luther! In these very different controversies the concept of the will was understood in terms of the specific psychological faculty of the willing subject.

The biblical usage, however, points unequivocally in a very different direction. The whole emphasis of *thelema* (will) in the New Testament falls on the content of the willing. Thus the concept of God's willing in particular is filled with content. We have here a warning against the abstract and undifferentiated use of the motif such as we met with above. Where and how do we encounter God's will? The Old Testament found it done in creation. It then saw it revealed in the history of Israel, and above all in the giving of the Law. The commanding word of the Lord played an important part as the instrument of his will. "By the word of the Lord the heavens were made, and all their host by the breath of his mouth. . . . For he spoke, and it came to be; he commanded, and it stood forth" (Ps. 33:6, 9). "Whatever the Lord pleases he does, in heaven and on earth, in the seas and all deeps" (Ps. 135:6). This usage is less common in the New Testament. It is true that the New Testament also knows that God's providence rules over all phenomena and events in the world. Not a sparrow falls to the ground "without your Father's will" (Matt. 10:29). Yet only in Revelation 4:11 is the concept of will related to creation: "Worthy art thou, our Lord and God, to receive glory and honor and power, for thou didst create all things, and by thy will they existed and were created."

Of narrower and more normative significance is the connection of the New Testament word with God's express will to save. We need note only that Matthew links the term consistently to God's title as Father (6:10; 7:21; 12:50; 18:14).[3] God's will is not an empty, generalized will. Its subject, the Father, orients it already. It is the will of the Father whose heart is clearly set on the salvation of his children. The Hebrew and Aramaic background is decisive at this point. The equivalents of *thelema* in these languages express the idea of good pleasure and even

3. See G. Schrenk, *TDNT,* 3:44ff.

joy. God's will is benevolent, not indifferent. Let us give some examples. The author of 1 Timothy 2:4 says categorically that God desires "all men to be saved and to come to the knowledge of the truth." Matthew 18:14 relates the will of God more narrowly to the destiny of the "little ones": "It is not the will of my Father who is in heaven that one of these little ones should perish." Similarly, in John 6:40 Christ, defining his mission, says that "this is the will of my Father, that every one who sees the Son and believes in him should have eternal life." Ephesians in hymnal form then sums it all up with reference to the whole cosmos: "He has made known to us in all wisdom and insight the mystery of his will . . . to unite all things in him, things in heaven and things on earth" (1:9-10).

Note that different witnesses and testimonies to God's will all look surprisingly in the same direction, that is, to our need of salvation. They begin concretely with the destiny of the little ones, with those to whom, according to the Gospel records, the promise of Jesus specifically applies. They then go further and think of the people of God, and yet also of Gentile peoples as well. They finally fix their gaze on the cosmos. This eschatologically oriented trend, eschatologically speeded up and crossing all frontiers, is intrinsic to the biblical concept of God's will. Hence the divine dynamic of salvation is the point of reference for the petition: "Thy will be done." We do not pray at random. We pray that the dynamic of salvation which is grounded in the will of God may work itself out in us, in our neighbors, and finally in all creation. In making the petition we say a committed yes to the eschatological and truly ecumenical will of God.

Incidentally, we should note here again that in the biblical text the verb comes before the subject, as in the first two petitions. It is hard to bring out this feature in translations, but we should at least respect the original emphasis. The petition has to do, not with a static state of affairs, but with a dynamic happening to which we relate ourselves, which we confess, and in the service of which we let ourselves be placed. In this connection Rudolf Bohren rightly speaks of a missionary petition. God's loving purposes, he maintains, embrace the whole world. His saving will embraces all humanity. On earth, then, the people of God is a people of mission or it is not God's people.[4]

The Wrestling of Jesus for the Father's Will

It is in the light of this concrete soteriological and eschatological filling out of the New Testament concept of God's will that we are to understand the New Testament story which has always played a special role in connection with this third petition: the story of Gethsemane (Matt. 26:36-46; cf. also Mark 14:32-42; Luke 22:40-46). The story is in some sense an authentic commentary of Jesus on his understanding of the petition. At the heart of it we find twice the same request, the second time in the same wording as that of the Lord's Prayer: "Thy will be done."

The context is important. Jesus is at the beginning of his Passion. He is clearly aware that his "hour" is near. In the biblical context this term applies not merely to the situation of suffering but to the final hour of eschatological decision. Jesus thus prepares for this hour of suffering and judgment. He does not do so as a composed philosopher. (We recall Socrates, who remained composed to the last as he made ready for death.) We see Jesus as an assailed and deeply troubled man: "My soul is very sorrowful, even to death" (Matt. 26:38). He seeks help from his brethren, and is disappointed. Above all, he brings his problem to the Father. (It is worth noting that here for the first time Mark uses the Aramaic *Abba*.) He does not suppress his own personal desire: "My Father, if it be possible, let this cup pass from me" (Matt. 26:39). The cup relates primarily to the human suffering connected with the Passion. Jesus is no masochist; he does not intentionally provoke suffering. He seeks if possible to avoid it. In the biblical context, however, the cup includes much more. It is the cup of eschatological judgment, of the wrath of God. This is how the prophets and psalmists understood it, and this

4. Bohren, *Unser Vater*, p. 63.

is how Jesus also understands it. This hour of his certainly means personal suffering but the suffering is also vicarious. It is an acceptance of eschatological judgment. This is the true seriousness and even terror of the decision that must be made.

It is in this situation that Jesus says: "Not as I will, but as thou wilt" (v. 39), and later, directly quoting the prayer he gave his disciples, "Thy will be done" (v. 42). We understand these words in the proper sense of the Gospels only if we do not construe the will of God abstractly and generally but concretely in the sense set forth above, that is, as the will that is oriented to the world's salvation. This is in accord with the whole thrust of the scene in Gethsemane. We have seen already that the event is full of soteriological and eschatological references. This is true especially of the central statements. Salvation in *judgment*, in the death of Jesus. For good reason the Son of Man trembles and is sorrowful, even to death. Yet *salvation* in judgment. With deadly seriousness the reconciliation and liberation of creation are at stake. Jesus cannot have the cup of salvation without the cup of judgment. So we say again, and with even greater emphasis, that here is the true seriousness and even terror of the decision which must be made. Will the bitter cup of salvation-judgment be filled and drained? Will Jesus, Son of his Father, draw back, or will he go his way, seeking and serving the Father's will to the bitter end? This is what Gethsemane is all about.

I stress the concrete setting and filling out of the "Thy will be done" of Gethsemane because otherwise we might misunderstand the story when seen as a commentary on the third petition of the Lord's Prayer. I have in mind especially the words: "Not as I will, but as thou wilt." How often this saying is quoted as a direction to unreserved acceptance of whatever comes, to a priori surrender of one's own will, as though we had here an ideology of submission. Along such lines the third petition is viewed too narrowly as a declaration that prepares us to bear situations of suffering. (Tertullian stated that in this saying we have an exhortation to bear suffering patiently.) We have seen, however, that as a commentary the Gethsemane story really points in a different direction. An active, not a passive Jesus comes before us in preparation for his Passion. He does not resignedly capitulate to the darkness that comes upon him. In spite of every threat he goes the way of salvation with a conscious act of will. Hence at the end of the scene he is not on his knees passively awaiting coming events. He stands up, rouses his disciples, and strides toward decision, going to meet this betrayer: "Rise, let us be going" (v. 46). Here, then, is confirmation: submission, but also resistance and even revolt is for Jesus part of the reality to which the petition "Thy will be done" bears reference.

A Polemical Thrust against Compartmentalizing

Let us tarry for a moment at the slogan: Revolt and resistance. What does it mean? Does it provide a basis for the thought of crusades? We know that on the margin this idea, too, might be viewed as one of the effects of the petition. "God wills it" was a cry which motivated the Christians who assembled in preparation for the Crusades. We have to accept the fact that activist as well as passivist misunderstandings—and the corresponding ideologies—have in fact resulted from the petition. We catch a glimpse of these even in Gethsemane: "And behold, one of those who were with Jesus stretched out his hand and drew his sword, and struck the slave of the high priest, and cut off his ear." But the reaction of Jesus was unmistakable: "Put your sword back into its place; for all who take the sword will perish by the sword" (Matt. 26:51-52). If we find revolt and resistance at the end of the story, it is clear that the real battle takes place within the one who prays. He is not resisting others but himself. It is he who must make the painful decision to serve the interests of the kingdom of God and not his own shortsighted interests.

This polemical aspect must have a place in our attempts to think and live in the light of the petition "Thy will be done." (As we noted earlier, the second petition, too, has a polemical edge in its opposition to our kingdoms.)

Martin Luther was one of the great expositors of the Lord's Prayer, and he laid special and even absolute emphasis on this polemical side. His whole exposition for simple laypeople (1519) centers on the theme that we hear something terrifying when we pray "Thy will be done."[5] For the simple fact that we must pray it daily shows that the will of God is not done among us. God's will is formulated in his commands. But in our own wills we ignore these commands. Our old Adam blatantly triumphs. Hence the third petition becomes judgment on him, in a radical sense. It calls for revolt and resistance against such tyranny, even for tyrannicide. As though the sharp controversy with Erasmus were already casting its shadow, Luther then considers the relation between God's will and ours. His answer is categorical: There is opposition between the two. Our will has to be broken, our good will as well as our evil, or secretly evil, will. For even our good will stands in God's way, making us self-willed and thus deaf to God's will. For self-will is the greatest and deepest evil in us, and nothing is dearer to us than our own will. Hence Luther can sum up the meaning of the third petition as follows: "In this petition you will notice that God bids us to pray against ourselves. In that way he teaches us that we have no greater enemy than ourself. . . . Therefore, we are asking for nothing else in this petition than the cross, torment, adversity, and sufferings of every kind, since these serve the destruction of our will."[6]

These statements of Luther are one-sided and exaggerated. In my view the basic theological weakness is that Luther seems here to take the will of God in a general sense and not in the New Testament sense of God's concrete will to save. As a result he tends to construe the relation between God's will and ours in a general sense as well, as an indifferent either-or, as though biblically there were no such thing as a will renewed by the Holy

---

5. Cf. "An Exposition of the Lord's Prayer for Simple Laymen, 1519," in *Luther's Works*, vol. 42: *Devotional Writings*, ed. Martin O. Dietrich, tr. Martin H. Bertram (Philadelphia: Fortress, 1969), p. 42.
6. Ibid., pp. 48-49.

Spirit in the life of faith. Perhaps the brewing clouds of the approaching storm of the debate with Erasmus about free will were already obscuring his vision. Calvin seemed to grasp the point more clearly when, elucidating the request in the *Institutes,* he noted: "Here it is not a question of his secret will, by which he controls all things and directs them to their end . . . . But here God's other will is to be noted—namely, that to which voluntary obedience corresponds."[7]

For all the objection to Luther's one-sidedness, however, it would be mistaken and foolish to set aside the core of his exposition. His polemical emphasis is right. Our petition has a critical edge—it has to have if it is prayed properly. It has a self-critical edge for those who pray it. It is a dangerous petition: it cost Jesus his life, and it cost his disciples a great deal. Considering God's will does not mean endorsing our open or secret wishes. It constantly cuts across them. It cuts across our good will as well as our evil will. We must take Luther seriously in this regard. It cuts across plans that we gladly approve and view as legitimate. We all have favored areas in which we would rather be on our own, autonomous, finding shelter from the will of God.

On this point I might refer to Walter Lüthi. "Our plight today consists in the fact that through fear of God's whole Will we prefer, so to speak, to 'go halves' with God time and again . . . . So we can divide ourselves into two or even three parts: we perhaps allow God to penetrate into our reason and our minds, but we are not prepared to give up our will to Him; that we want to keep to ourselves. As a result we have that lukewarm Christianity, that mediocre, half or two-thirds Christianity that is only too familiar to us. That is what Christianity is suffering from."[8]

The arts of compartmentalizing have been with Christianity throughout its history, especially in the Constantinian era. Virtuosity has been achieved in them and countless strategies

---

7. Calvin, *Institutes,* 2:906, § 3.20.43.
8. Lüthi, *Lord's Prayer,* p. 35.

have been tried. The underlying thrust is usually the same, namely, to divide up the reality of life and to exclude God's will (his saving will) from certain spheres. They vary according to priorities. An example from our own time comes to mind. For centuries the Sermon on the Mount has been, if not flatly contested, at least immunized as regards political and social life. The slogan is that one cannot govern with the Sermon on the Mount. The politico-economic sphere has its own laws and forces that one has to respect. How many personally devout people have thus shut out the petition for God's saving will (as exemplified in the Sermon on the Mount) from these areas.

Today many Christians have a clearer vision in this respect. The will and righteousness of God do not come to a halt before the problems of social life, even the difficult problems of structures. The demands for righteousness, peace, and freedom relate to the question of the ensemble of social relations (Marx), of the economic and political system. Christians who are involved here from the standpoint of theology and social ethics are rightly correcting the arts of compartmentalizing in this area. Yet is it not true that among such people the threat of new arts may be seen at various points? Because they view the question of the system, of great structures, as decisive, do they undervalue that of a readiness for personal sacrifice, of private life-style? A conversation with the president of a church council gave me something to think about. "Yes, yes," he said, "it is our socially involved pastors who make the biggest private claims." We must not make of this statement a generalization. Yet it illustrates the temptation which reached a cynical peak in the notorious saying of a pretentious radical socialist: "Comrades, the way of socialism is hard. Let us enjoy the fruits of withering capitalism."

The petition "Thy will be done" contradicts the arts of compartmentalizing, whether ecclesiastical or secular, whether social or private. It relates to the totality, seeking to renew both the heart and the world of those who pray it. It applies especially to sectors that are particularly important to us and that thus represent particular temptations in terms of our own disposition, interests, or position, that is, to areas in which we would like to be left undisturbed on our own. It is precisely in these areas that the third petition of the Lord's Prayer is to be heard, prayed, and practiced: "Thy will be done, on earth as it is in heaven."

Emulating the Heavenly State

It is now time to discuss the second part of the petition: "On earth as it is in heaven." Some commentators point out that this clause applies not only here but also by way of expansion and background to the first two petitions as well: "Hallowed be thy name, on earth as it is in heaven"; "Thy kingdom come, on earth as in heaven." Origen proposed this interpretation, and the Catechism of Trent (1566) has a pastoral direction along these lines.[9] The idea is theologically important and is surely in keeping with the intention of Jesus. The name, the kingdom, and the will of God relate to the total reality of creation.

Yet in the text the thought actually occurs only in connection with the third petition. In some manuscripts, especially Codex D, the word *hos* ("as") is left out. This opens up the possibility that God's will has yet to be done in heaven as well as on earth, as though Christ's saving work were still incomplete in heaven. But most manuscripts include "as" and thus suggest a different possibility of interpretation.

In the Bible and the Creed heaven and earth denote the whole creation. They are not polar opposites. They belong to the one reality that was originally good and that is sustained by God's creative will. They are related to one another and ordered to one another. Yet there is a clear distinction between heaven and earth. Heaven is the sphere that we human beings can neither see nor control. Earth is entrusted to us for our responsible and accountable government. Even more decisively from the standpoint of the text, relations in heaven and on earth

9. Cf. J. Carmignac, *Recherches sur le "Notre Père"* (Paris: Letouzey, 1969), pp. 112-13.

are very different. On earth there is opposition to God's will as Creator. We go our own way and in our alienation we disrupt the order of the creation entrusted to us, desecrating God's name and building our evil empires. "All have turned aside, together they have gone wrong; no one does good, not even one" (Rom. 3:12, quoting Ps. 14:3). In heaven, however, there is already conformity to God's will. God finds there already what he is seeking on earth—faith, the yes of his creation, the praise of the heavenly hosts.

When, therefore, we pray "Thy will be done, on earth as it is in heaven," this means praying that heavenly relations may become earthly relations, that the heavenly today may be the earthly tomorrow which with Christ's coming has dawned already in his name and kingdom. The church father Chrysostom was thus biblically right when he commented: "May we, Lord, emulate the heavenly state, making his will ours."[10] The heavenly state, the coming city of God, the New Jerusalem, is to be a paradigm for our earthly cities. As in the Bohemian Reformation, we must respond already to this eschatological reality with an initiative of faith, love, and hope.

This ordering of earth to heaven in the one—new—creation is the point of the third petition of the Lord's Prayer, and not of this alone but of the first two as well. Naturally, this does not mean that we are to try fanatically to build heaven on earth according to our own plan and will. As is well known, such attempts have always led to a perverted hell on earth. What the petition requires is that we should engage in prayer to God that also commits us to action. Thus we must pray with the prophet the Advent prayer: "O that thou wouldst rend the heavens and come down, that the mountains might quake at thy presence—as when fire kindles brushwood and the fire causes water to boil—to make thy name known to thy adversaries" (Isa. 64:1-2). It is for this that we pray with Jesus when we say: "Thy will be done, on earth as it is in heaven."

10. Cf. Lohmeyer, "Lord's Prayer," p. 128.

Give Us This Day
Our Daily Bread

The Threshold in the Prayer

At the end of his discussion of the fourth petition, Lohmeyer said that this petition is the heart and center of the Lord's Prayer.[1] This statement is theologically important from the standpoint of both its form and its content. The petition is indeed central. It brings us to a threshold. The second part of the text begins with it. In a certain sense it functions like a railway switch or turntable. What do we mean?

We detect the threshold as soon as we look at it or hear it. We have only to note the pronouns. Thus far the Lord's Prayer (after the invocation) has had "thy": *thy* name, *thy* kingdom, *thy* will. But now we find a repeated "our": *our* bread, *our* debts, *our* temptation, *our* being menaced by evil. The change is unmistakable. If his cause, God's cause, was foremost in the first part, our cause is foremost in the second.

We should not overestimate the height of this threshold. It does not check the movement. It is not an invincible barrier or a break. The Lord's Prayer is not changing themes. In the

1. Lohmeyer, *"Lord's Prayer,"* p. 159.

deepest sense every petition in it has to do with human need. To anticipate, we might say, too, that a methodological feature of the second part is that every petition has to do with God's honor. This dialectic, this shifting of perspectives, is deeply anchored in the structure, in the spirit of the biblical message. God's movement with us is the central thought of the Old Testament and also of the New, in which it takes the final shape of witness to the divine incarnation. Here is the cantus firmus of the biblical message with its many and varied voices. In the fourth petition of the Lord's Prayer, then, we have a shift of perspective, not of theme. That is why I speak of a railway switch or turntable which we now reach and cross.

With this caveat, however, I still insist that we will find the threshold or switch not merely in the formal sense indicated by the change of pronouns but also concretely, as we see in the first petition of the second part: "Give us this day our daily bread." When it comes to petitions relating to specifically human need, we pray first for bread. This is surprising. The contrast is incomparably great. To the glory of the divine themes—God's name, kingdom, and will—it would seem that primarily on the human side the religious themes—forgiveness of debts, victory over temptation, and deliverance from evil—would correspond much better than the banal and everyday request for bread. Ebeling might well ask what room there is between the eternal God and our ultimate future for this almost petty attention to transitory and unimportant everyday things, and even more surprisingly to the paltry daily ration that we need to eke out life from today to tomorrow.[2]

It is no wonder that in the history of exposition a strong group, ranging from Origen to the younger Luther and on to our own day, has favored a spiritualizing interpretation, taking bread in a spiritual sense as God's Word or Christ's mystical body. This interpretation has behind it serious biblical and theological arguments that we shall have to discuss. But to regard

---

2. G. Ebeling, *On Prayer: The Lord's Prayer in Today's World*, tr. James W. Leitch (Philadelphia: Fortress, repr. 1978), p. 52.

them as decisive and to choose the spiritualizing option as the most obvious one seems to me to be impermissible both biblically and theologically. Martin Luther was right when in the course of his theological development he gave up the spiritualizing understanding of the petition and like John Calvin in his *Institutes* and catechisms he began his exposition with our concrete needs, especially finely and effectively in the well-known formulation in his Small Catechism. Asking what is meant by daily bread, he relates it to everything pertaining to the nourishment and needs of the body, eating, drinking, clothes, shoes, houses, farms, fields, cattle, money, goods, good and devout spouses, devout children, devout and faithful rulers, good government, good weather, peace, health, discipline, honor, good friends, trusty neighbors, and the like.[3]

Holy Materialism

Why in our exposition do we think it theologically and ethically advisable to take "bread" so decidedly in the literal, earthly, bodily sense? I will give three reasons.

(1) Let us deal first with the obvious and, to many people, disturbing contrast between the loftiness of the first motifs, God's name, kingdom, and will, and the banal pettiness of the earthly problems bound up with the term "bread." The contrast is not so great as is at first thought. We have only to recall our expositions of the first three petitions. In all of them we came up against a common tendency, namely, that the prayer in no way takes us out of very concrete everyday life. On the contrary, in their implications the first three petitions reach into the earthly conditions of our lives. We pray for the hallowing of God's name, not in heaven, but here on earth. The kingdom of God is

3. *Die Bekenntnisschriften der Evangelisch-Lutherischen Kirche*, 3rd ed. (Göttingen: Vandenhoeck & Ruprecht, 1956), p. 514; cf. P. Schaff, *The Creeds of Christendom*, 4th ed. (New York: Harper & Brothers, 1919), 3:82-83.

not of this world, yet its coming unquestionably calls for conversion and faith and hence for our confronting of the world's
actual conditions with the promises. The will of God has to do
with earth as well as heaven. The last phrase must be taken with
full seriousness: on earth as in heaven. Note that the final words
of the first half relate to earth. If the second half begins with
bread, this confirms the fact that the contrast is not all that great.
God's will for our earth is also, and perhaps first of all, that there
should be bread—earthly, everyday bread corresponding to the
conditions of earth.

(2) The concrete reference finds support when we consider the specifically biblical way of thinking. The Bible recognizes no rigid dualism of heaven and earth, body and soul,
time and eternity. Dualistic thinking has dominated broad
stretches of the history of religion and philosophy. I have in
mind the higher religions of India and those of the Near East,
or especially the metaphysical tradition of antiquity that has
had such an influence on us. The idealistically oriented peren-
nial philosophy did its thinking under the control of spiritualist axioms. True reality transcends the corporeal and earthly.
It lies in the world of spirit and ideas. A corresponding anthropological consequence is the one-sided advocacy of soul
against body. Metaphysical salvation is for the soul alone. The
body is a prison of the soul (soma—sema), and if possible we
must vanquish and discard it.

The Bible contradicts the idealistic, spiritualist axiom. It
does so in every respect—cosmologically, anthropologically,
and eschatologically—and with all the ethical implications.
God's good creation embraces heaven and earth: "In the beginning God created the heavens and the earth" (Gen. 1:1). God's
creation is a totality. The earth, especially the earth, gives us a
good start in life. And we too, as body and soul, or spirit, soul,
and body, are a psychosomatic unity and totality, not a divided
phenomenon. Metaphysical, or, better, eschatological hope is
not just for heaven but for the new heaven and the new earth.
So far as we are concerned, it is not for the immortality of the

soul but, as the Creed provocatively puts it, for the resurrection of the flesh.[4]

On this basis the Bible exhorts us to champion the right of the earth, which theology thus far has largely ignored, but which, because of the ecological crisis, has now become one of the foremost tasks of today and tomorrow. It also bids us champion the rights of the body. Throughout church history, it is true, the church has largely neglected these motifs, undoubtedly due in part to the influence of the idealistic axiom, which Christian theology adopted so quickly and uncritically. Yet especially on the left wing of church history a biblically better insight continually found expression. As is well known, Oetinger stated that "corporeality is the end of all God's ways"—a thesis which, though deliberately exaggerated, rests on a good theological foundation in view of the thrust of biblical thinking, and especially in view of the central biblical message of the incarnation of the Word (John 1:14).

Consistently in the recent history of exposition we find the slogan "holy materialism," for example, in Leonhard Ragaz and other Religious Socialists. Naturally, this does not mean that we are to set an undifferentiated materialism in opposition to an undifferentiated idealism, nor that materialism as a system is to be called holy. That would hardly be a more innocuous misunderstanding than the first one. The term "holy" is used to qualify rather than to transfigure the meaning of materialism in this context. As Ragaz said, matter, too, is God's creation. It is sanctified to him. It belongs to him. It must serve and glorify him.[5] As regards our understanding of the petition "Give us this day our daily bread," this means that the question of bread in its literal sense by no means covers the full horizon of the fourth petition, let alone of the Lord's Prayer as a whole. Jesus himself plainly refutes such an idea: "Man shall not live by bread alone,

4. Cf. my work *The Faith We Confess: An Ecumenical Dogmatics*, tr. David Lewis (Philadelphia: Fortress, 1984), pp. 236ff.
5. Ragaz, "Das Unservater," p. 17.

but by every word that proceeds out of the mouth of God" (Matt. 4:4). Yet every word, including every word that proceeds out of the mouth of God, has to do with matter too, with concrete earthly questions and answers. Thus the fourth petition in the literal sense is at the heart of the Lord's Prayer.

(3) The Bible's high regard for eating, for meals, suggests to me that it is wise to begin with a literal understanding of bread in trying to interpret the Lord's Prayer. Already in the Old Testament, eating bread and having meals were not only necessary to life but also provided opportunity for refreshing human contacts.

The same is true in the New Testament, especially in the Synoptic Gospels. We must not overlook the part played by the meal, especially the common meal, in the history of Jesus. For those outside, it marked his life-style. Unlike the ascetic John the Baptist, Jesus appeared to friend and foe alike as "a glutton and a drunkard" (Matt. 11:19). He was critically opposed to an ascetic life-style. Table fellowship in particular was vitally important to him: among his disciples as a seal of brotherhood; yet also, in his unreserved readiness to eat with tax collectors and sinners, as an understandable way (though the righteous misunderstood it) of showing the solidarity of God's love with people near and distant. On good grounds one might say that this table fellowship, practiced in various ways, is a feature of the whole message of Jesus. When he himself said: "I am among you as one who serves" (Luke 22:27), the original sense is that he is there as a waiter at table. He sees to it that people are fed, as one notes, for example, in the story of the miraculous feeding of the thousands. Even in relation to our final hope he uses images drawn from table fellowship, though now he transcends, but does not wholly eliminate, the literal sense of eating bread. We see this in the many parables of the kingdom of God as a feast, or, with reference to other peoples, in the promise: "Many will come from east and west and sit at table with Abraham, Isaac, and Jacob in the kingdom of heaven" (Matt. 8:11).

It was no doubt recollection of the importance of eating bread for Jesus, even in the sense of meeting material needs, that led the first disciples to take effective measures to care especially for the needy, for example, widows, lest any should be in economic want. We may also recall the setting up of the ministry of deacons as one of the first offices in the primitive church, with oversight of the distribution of bread as their specific task. Thus one of the very earliest Christian structures was created to deal with this concern, the sharing and distributing of daily bread. Obviously, the question of material bread is not marginal but central in the church's activity and prayers. The petition for bread rightly lies at the heart of the Lord's Prayer.

Biblical Bread

Let us now turn more precisely to the three terms in the petition. (1) We have already said something about the central motif, "bread" *(artos)*. I would only add that bread is a many-faceted concept in the Bible. In the New Testament we can distinguish three related layers of meaning.[6]

The first reference is to bread in the elementary sense, the common staple of life made from wheat which is baked, distributed, and eaten to appease hunger. The typical situation of eating bread is often linked to the role of the father or host who "at the beginning of a meal takes bread, gives thanks, breaks it and gives to those at table with him."[7] The New Testament repeatedly depicts a scene of this kind, whether in everyday life or at the Last Supper and even in a meeting with the Risen Lord (cf. Mark 6:41 par.; 14:22 par.; Luke 24:30). Paul as well as Jesus acts in this way. At a critical hour in his life, in mortal peril during the storm at sea, he encourages his panic-stricken companions by urging them to take bread: "And when he had said this, he took bread, and giving thanks to God in the presence of all he broke it and began to eat" (Acts 27:35).

Second, bread in New Testament usage, as also in ours, is

---

6. As J. Behm does in *TDNT*, 1:477-78.
7. Ibid., p. 477.

not just bread in the narrow sense but also nourishment in general. The same is true of the Hebrew *lehem* and the Aramaic *lahma*. Paul has this in view when he tells the Thessalonians to work quietly and eat their own bread (i.e., earn their own living, 2 Thess. 3:12). They are not to live at the expense of others, eating others' bread without paying (v. 8). Against the temptation to be idle he issues the stern warning: "If any one will not work, let him not eat" (v. 10). In this context "bread" stands for the necessities of life.

Third, the motif also carries with it another sense that is not literal or earthly. Bread symbolizes the heavenly, eschatological banquet. In the introduction to the parable of the great feast we read: "Blessed is he who shall eat bread in the kingdom of God" (Luke 14:15). This is a promise that also lies behind the Last Supper that Jesus eats with his disciples. John in particular takes up the motif in an eschatological, sacramental sense. Jesus himself is here identified as the true bread from heaven (John 6:31ff.). "I am the living bread which came down from heaven; if any one eats of this bread, he will live for ever" (v. 51). Even though we may be convinced that in the fourth petition of the Lord's Prayer "bread" is not to be taken, at least primarily, in this third, heavenly sense, it is important not simply to lose sight of this layer. In the New Testament the three layers are very closely related and are "pervious" to one another, so that we must not play them off against each other. The fact that they are pervious will occupy us later in connection with spiritualizing interpretations of the petition, which mostly appeal to the third layer.

(2) The word "daily" presents us with a truly knotty point of interpretation: "Give us this day our *daily* bread." The Greek word, found in both Matthew and Luke, is *epiousios*. The almost insuperable difficulty is that the word is a hapax legomenon, that is, it occurs only here in the Greek Bible and indeed in Greek literature as a whole. Origen already pointed out that the word was unknown either in literary or in popular speech. It is true that another example has now been found but it is by no means unequivocal (an incomplete word, which can be reconstructed to *epiousion*, has been found on a 5th-

century papyrus from Upper Egypt; in a list of expenses, it denotes the daily ration).

The occurrence of an unknown word in the Lord's Prayer is a real puzzle. As Lohmeyer said, "In a prayer which is intended for daily use and which deals with the simplest and deepest matters of human life and divine action, in a prayer which is as clear and brief as it is close knit and comprehensible, we find a Greek word which occurs here for the first time and which for a number of centuries occurred only here."[8] In such circumstances one may easily see why many proposals and possibilities of interpretation have arisen during the history of exposition. I will mention three.

Epiousios is commonly taken to mean "for tomorrow." Jerome inclines in this direction, arguing that the Aramaic Gospel of the Hebrews has *mahar*. In this case we are praying that God will give us today bread for tomorrow. But this rendering brings us into some tension with another saying of Jesus that is quite close in the Sermon on the Mount: "Do not be anxious about tomorrow" (Matt. 6:34). Other expositors have given "tomorrow" a transferred sense and seen a reference to the eschatological last day. Bread is then quite logically given a spiritual meaning. It is heavenly, metaphysical bread, the bread of the kingdom of God. In church history the Vulgate directed theologians along this path by translating the word as *supersubstantialis* in Matthew, though astonishingly it has *cotidianus* in Luke. This rendering gives free play to metaphysical sacramental thinking that is totally alien to the original text.

Modern commentators incline more, though not exclusively, to a third possibility. They see in *epiousios* an indication of measure rather than of time. Jesus is teaching his disciples to be satisfied, not to want superfluity, not to seek long-term security, not to heap up goods, but to ask only for what is necessary and sufficient for the day. This is in keeping not only with that other, if foreign, secular finding on the Egyptian papyrus ("daily ration"), but also with the attitude of Old Testament wisdom,

8. Lohmeyer, *"Lord's Prayer,"* pp. 145-46.

91

which was aware of threats on two sides: that of bitter need but also the temptation of excess. Hence the devout prayer of Proverbs: "Give me neither poverty nor riches; feed me with the food that is needful for me, lest I be full, and deny thee, and say, 'Who is the Lord,' or lest I be poor, and steal, and profane the name of my God" (Prov. 30:8-9). Along these lines a meaningful translation might be: "Give us this day the bread that we need."[9]

(3) This understanding seems to me to find confirmation when we turn to the expression "this day." In both versions it comes at the end, but in two forms: Luke has *kath'hemeran* ("day by day"), Matthew the shorter and categorical *semeron* ("today"). Some commentators want to take this "today" eschatologically as the "today" of the coming kingdom of God, and not without good reason. The whole preaching and work of Jesus stand under the sign of such a "today," as we see from his first sermon at Nazareth (Luke 4:21). This view in no way devalues the everyday sense of the disciples' "today" as spoken in the prayer. The shortened perspective of the time of God teaches us to accept the limited time of earthly life. We are not to hoard or heap up life's bread. It is sufficient, and must be sufficient, for the span of the "today" entrusted to us.

In this connection I am reminded of the story of the manna in the Old Testament (Exod. 16). Again and again commentaries on this petition have rightly recalled it. It has a point that none can miss; manna cannot be hoarded. It is enough for the day, for the short "today" of our pilgrimage. In spite of that, or, better, because of it, it is a sign of the grace that is ever new. This point applies also to our daily bread. The fourth petition of the Lord's Prayer, relating with special emphasis to the concrete needs of human life, sets our human existence in a sober but liberating and gracious light.

Human need is set in the light of the petition for bread. In closing let us now try to take up this theme in three trains of thought: Hungry Humanity, Bread and Justice, and God and Bread.

9. On this whole question cf. W. Foerster in *TDNT*, 2:590-99.

Hungry Humanity

In the light of the petition, humanity is seen basically to be hungry, to be dependent constantly on bread, to be needy. As Gerhard Ebeling put it, "like all living things [man] is a hungering being. Living and being in need are one and the same thing. We are in a bad way when we cannot satisfy our hunger. But we are in an equally bad way when we no longer feel any hunger. . . . The stomach demands its daily rights. Even all of man's great achievements by which human power and riches are unfolded in the economic and technical world, in civilization and culture, have behind them the active urges that spring from man's indigence. However high he climbs in the spiritual world, man remains dependent on the material nurture of his body."[10]

The biblical view of humanity takes this elemental human condition very seriously. I referred earlier to the holy materialism of the prophetic and apostolic message. We must now develop this thought as follows. Humanity's material needs must never be underestimated. They have their rights and dignity on the basis of God's good creation. Taken from the earth, we are earthly creatures. God has given us the earth and its material powers and resources. We depend on them. We need not be ashamed of this dependence. We need not keep quiet about it or repress it. We are body as well as soul, with all that this implies. We have impulses, needs, and material interests. To have no material needs is not in itself an ideal. In this regard the Bible parts company with many religions and philosophical trends in which asceticism plays a decisive role. Diogenes with his program of setting aside every need is no saint, no model of Christian piety, even though he might have found many admirers and disciples in church history, especially in monastic circles. Asceticism as an end in itself is not a biblical way. Our vital interests have their rights and dignity.

In the context of human life before God, however, the fourth petition of the Lord's Prayer defines not only the worth

10. Ebeling, *On Prayer*, p. 57.

of material needs but also their comparative worth. At this point we must allow for the opposing emphasis. More common perhaps than the first case is a second misunderstanding of material interests in human life: an overvaluing of them rather than an undervaluing. As things are, or, to put it theologically, under the sign of the Fall, human needs have a notorious tendency to grow, to grow to excess. There is a legitimate hunger in the interests of self-preservation. There is also a perverted hunger that is oriented to accumulation and growth and that knows no bounds. There is the hunger for power. Human drives, including the sex drive in distinction from this drive in other creatures, often go beyond what is in keeping with creation. In principle at least they become insatiable. Material interests take over the heart and become idols.

The petition sets clear limits to this temptation that bedazzles us. "Give us this day our daily bread": the two expressions that we have already discussed, "daily" and "this day," point in this direction. They limit the question of bread even as they take it seriously both quantitatively and qualitatively. They put what is essential to life in the center: our daily bread today. They set the corresponding priorities. Those who pray this prayer must also set them. This means that we may not put anything we please under the protection and promise of the Lord's Prayer. In the history of exposition and in many sermons on the fourth petition one may detect a tendency in this direction, even in the best commentators. I recall the fine saying in Luther's Small Catechism in which he lists under "daily bread" not merely nourishment but houses, farms, fields, wives, families, health, and honor. I think that this is basically right, yet it opens the door to misunderstanding. It is as though we could set an extensive list of needs under the petition for bread and in this way justify them. The brief and sober wording of the petition—especially the "daily" and "this day"—counsels restraint as regards this tendency toward free expansion.

Thus in praying the prayer we must show not only our freedom as regards material needs but also our readiness to test them critically, not to let them grow excessively, not to fall victim to them. Jesus was well aware of the latter temptation. We need only think of the parable of the rich farmer (Luke 12:16ff.). This man died because of his obsession with the question of bread. He died both in time and eternity. For, as Jesus said pointedly, "Man shall not live by bread alone" (Matt. 4:4). Criticism of needs and interests is required.

This criticism was always required, but it is urgently required today. For in distinction from past epochs in world history, we industrialized countries have reached a stage when elemental needs are for the first time met, or, as we might say more cautiously, can be met. We live in a society of superfluity. An unchecked thirst for ever more striking luxuries and their shameless display has recently put forth its artificially cultivated blossoms. It is no accident that the theme of luxury has become a central one in the press, not merely relative to the life-style of the rich and famous, but also relative to the prevailing morality of the age.

Has it brought with it a leap from the realm of necessity to that of freedom? At first sight it might seem so to an observer from past centuries. Much has been achieved compared to the elementary conditions of life that obtained for our ancestors. Yet most of us know better. In relation to our society we cannot speak of the realm of freedom in the full sense. Our realm of freedom is at the same time a realm of new compulsions. Many of these are linked to the excessive, artificially provoked, and manipulated needs of our consumer society. They do not make us freer or richer. At the cost of our true human and co-human needs, they make us poorer and more dependent.

The prayer for bread in the Lord's Prayer ought to make us rethink the situation. It should do so in the personal sphere by encouraging us freely to restrict our needs. We must positively accept ascetic impulses. Let us not forget that in the Sermon on the Mount something is said about fasting (Matt. 6:16ff.). Naturally, asceticism will not be an end in itself; it will be a tool in the urgent clarifying of priorities. It will accomplish this in the area of thought by encouraging the church's theology to submit the ideologies and strategies of need in our consumer society to a critical test. It will accomplish it also in social ethics by working out the social dimension of the question of bread and emphasizing it. This brings us to our second heading in the present discussion.

Bread and Justice

In our commentary thus far on the fourth petition we have not mentioned one little word that appears in two forms. It is the pronoun "us" and "our." We must not overlook it, for it draws our attention to a central point. We do not ask for ourselves alone but in a human fellowship. The bread that we pray for is concretely and expressly our bread, but from the standpoint of the preceding petitions, especially the prayer for God's kingdom, it is not ours alone. It is our common bread that we share with others. The question of justice—along with that of bread and from the standpoint of God's kingdom—is at the heart of the Lord's Prayer. The bread of the fourth petition is bread that must be shared.

It is noteworthy how often and emphatically in the Old Testament already the motif of bread is linked to the command to share. Thus we read in Isa. 58:7: "Share your bread with the hungry." The psalmist, too, praises God as the one "who executes justice for the oppressed, who gives food to the hungry" (Ps. 146:7). The impressive references to the hungry and oppressed, and the emphatic word "justice," cannot be excluded from any theologically responsible discussion of the petition for bread, and certainly not in any circumstances today. For the nub of the problem is that there are hungry people in our world, masses of them. This is true at a time when, as noted, in vast areas of the world the question of bread is to a large extent detached from the context of physical hunger. In this situation of sharp contrast the words "right" and "justice" have a special force that must very deeply affect Christians who pray the Lord's Prayer. There is something very wrong about our handling of bread if near and far millions of hungry people are watching our mountains of bread and butter constantly growing.

Today, especially in so-called better circles, a new use has been found for the word "sin," which otherwise occurs only infrequently. After lavish meals people say: "I have sinned today." What they mean is that they have sinned against their waistline. Against their better judgment they have put on too many pounds. But this word, which in the first instance is uttered complacently, jokingly, and with patting of a well-filled stomach, might well take a serious and ominous turn. Extravagant consumption, not only of foods but also of other basic raw materials, might become a real sin against our needy fellows and against God, and hence it might also become a judgment. Conversion is needed.

In these circumstances the prayer for bread becomes a word of conversion. It sharpens our eyes and consciences to the rights of the hungry and oppressed. Even little steps count. The Reformation in its day, for good reasons, objected to fasting as a religious exercise and an act of self-righteousness. But the situation has now changed. It might be that in view of the deadly contrast between superfluity and hunger in our modern world a readiness to fast will again become a sign of freedom, not as a duty or a strenuous achievement, but in free turning to the needs of others and thus in orientation, not to one's own perfection, but to the rights of the hungry, as a sign of a readiness to share and in recognition that "our daily bread" in the Lord's Prayer means bread for our brothers and sisters as well.

"Bread for Brothers" is fittingly the title of an annual ecumenical Swiss collection on behalf of the Third World. Here in fact, face to face with the need of bread in our modern world, Christian philanthropy, the demonstration of practical love of neighbor, is demanded. At the heart of our praying, and also, of course, of our readiness to give practical help, the work of relief must be taken up and supported. Even small steps count.

But the scope of the petition is broader. The issue is not just one of private renunciation and benevolence, though these are not to be disparaged as obligatory marks of conversion. Under the conditions of our one world, which is increasingly brought closer together in mutual involvement and dependence, we have also to put the urgent question of the order or system under the sign of which hunger arises and the disproportion between different countries grows. The Religious Socialists already saw clearly that the Lord's Prayer must be applied in this area that seems to be dominated by forces that are hard to change. Leonhard Ragaz pointed out that in asking for daily bread we ask for change in the modern social order, which rests on exploitation and profit. We ask for the overcoming of greed and fear, for fair pay for fair work, for the ending of unemployment, for the disappearance of alcoholism and prostitution, for the saving of nature from destruction by a technology that works in the service of false gods.[11]

For decades thinking has been moving in this direction, first (in the forties and fifties) under the slogan "responsible society" (with a predominantly Western orientation), then after 1966, as Christians from the Third World became increasingly involved, under the slogan "responsible world society." Today we discuss models of a new society, and ways to it, under the slogan "just, sustainable, and participating society." Note the predicates. The economic order must be just but also sustainable (embracing the environment that is threatened with destruction). Above all, it must be oriented to participation and sharing. Is the ecumenical movement becoming involved in side issues in this regard? I think not, so long as it maintains a theological perspective, reflects and acts in a differentiated way, and avoids ideological shortcuts. The fourth petition encourages us to take steps in this direction. As a Latin American prayer puts it, "O God, to those who have hunger give bread; and to those who have bread the hunger for justice."[12]

11. Ragaz, "Das Unservater," p. 19.
12. Quoted by Krister Stendahl, "Your Kingdom Come," *Cross Currents* 32/3 (1982) 263.

God and Bread

To pray "Give us this day our daily bread" is to confess that God and bread belong inseparably together, whether the movement be from God to bread or from bread to God. Thus far we have been looking in the first direction. God comes into the question of bread and his justice applies there. Let us now stress the other aspect. When we receive, we eat our bread before God. The fourth petition of the Lord's Prayer and the whole Bible, especially the Old Testament, teach us to value bread as a good gift of God. True, bread is also a product of human hands, the result of economic activity. For biblical faith, however, it is at the same time infinitely more; it is a proof of the goodness of the Creator.

From the standpoint of the Lord's Prayer, then, the question of bread is not just an economic matter. It is also a theological matter and primarily a doxological matter. In the Bible praise and thanksgiving constantly ring out for daily bread, for ours and for the food given to our fellows and to fellow creatures. The words of the psalmist are unforgettable: "The eyes of all look to thee, and thou givest them their food in due season. Thou openest thy hand, thou satisfiest the desire of every living thing" (Ps. 145:15-16). A Jewish grace from the time of Jesus is to the same effect: "Praised be thou, O Lord our God, king of the world, who dost feed the whole world by thy goodness. In grace, love, and mercy he gives bread to all flesh . . . For he feeds and provides for all and shows his kindness to all and assigns food to all his creatures which he has made. Praised be thou, Lord, who dost feed all."[13]

In such texts, for which the New Testament has parallels in various contexts, two emphases stand out. First, they portray God as a generous Creator and extol him as a Giver of bread. He grants food not just to those who have merited it but to all. We recall the saying of Jesus in Matthew 5:45 that the sun shines on the bad as well as the good and the rain refreshes all. Fundamen-

13. Cf. P. Billerbeck, *Kommentar zum NT aus Talmud und Midrasch* (Munich: Beck'sche, 1928), 6:531.

tally, God's righteousness is not oriented to work or merit; it is rich in grace. This is worth noting, with all its ramifications. In a humanitarian society the question of bread cannot take the rigid form of a question of mere achievement. It is true that in everyday life in society we can hardly avoid evaluating achievement. We need the carrot and the stick if we are to focus our gifts and forces, to mobilize them and put them to use. But before God the mentality and society of achievement find their limits. They do so concretely in the matter of bread. Bread—that is, the elemental conditions of life—must be made available, so far as possible, to all. Various measures that are being taken in East and West to achieve this goal are steps in the right direction.

The second emphasis is that if bread and God belong together, then for us bread and thanksgiving belong together. The texts already quoted are thanksgivings, graces. The people of the Bible, and devout people in all ages, realize that we cannot take bread for granted. This fact bitterly confronts them in experiences of want and hunger. From a vertical standpoint (i.e., in relation to God), bread ultimately comes from God. It is a sign and gift of his grace. Recollection of the story of the manna offers an illustration. The first thing we ought to do when we take bread, even before eating, is to give thanks, to say grace.

Grace! What has become of it today? Werner Pfendsack, onetime pastor at Basel Minster, said in his exposition of the Lord's Prayer that our parents and grandparents still said grace, but as the children grew older the day came when they acknowledged their ingratitude by abandoning grace. Instead of recalling the miracle of daily bread, we no longer pray or give thanks at meals. This is how it has gone. No wonder that the family has ceased to be a place of meeting and has become instead the place of cheap and often fractious lodging.[14]

We are probably tempted to dismiss this matter as nostalgic. But more is at stake than the fine habit of saying grace or table manners in general. (It should be noted that in our lands of overabundance there is vacillation between the two extremes

14. Pfendsack, *Unser Vater* (Basel: 1961), p. 57.

of fast food, hasty eating with no social contact, and lavish display, meaningless and unworthy excess. Both fall short in terms not merely of human culture but also of the dignity of bread as the good gift of God.) From the standpoint of the spirit of prayer we must handle bread differently, namely, with glad thankfulness and respect.

The Czech language has a fine term for bread which was earlier used as an equivalent for grace in popular speech: *boží dar*, God's gift, often in the diminutive with a suggestion of tenderness, *boží dárek* (which is very hard to translate). Thus if a piece of bread fell from the table in peasants' houses, the custom was to lift it up very carefully and to kiss it reverently.

Now in saying this I am not calling for compulsory grace or for training in the kissing of bread. What I am asking for is reflection on the essential point that the inseparable relation between God and bread brings before us, namely, that we cannot take bread for granted, or, to put it positively, that we must learn to eat bread thankfully. We do not live by bread alone. This statement also means that the mere eating of bread, without gratitude and in detachment from God and neighbor, cannot be a means of blessing to us. We die by bread alone. This is a danger that threatens to destroy us both morally and socially in our society of overabundance, whether before God or our hungry fellows. To take things for granted in our dealings with bread, to have the lack of gratitude and respect that may be seen in our madness of consumption and waste—these things attack at the roots today a "just, sustainable, and participatory society." Here again we must say that conversion is needed. To pray "Give us this day our daily bread" is for us the beginning of revolt against this disorder in the world.

Eucharistic Implications

In the history of the ecumenical church we find a rich tradition that might help us to conversion and to a deeper understanding of the question of bread. This is the eucharistic tradition. We will turn to it as we close this attempt to interpret the fourth petition.

Let us survey our train of thought thus far. In seeking to understand this petition, we have decided for a holy materialism, for an earthly, material approach and perspective. Yet we have also mentioned that another strand in the history of exposition pleads—in part on good biblical grounds—for a spiritual interpretation of daily bread.

What are the spiritual motifs which led so many thinkers in this direction, from Origen, by way of the whole Middle Ages, to our own day? There are above all two incontestable biblical emphases. The first is the strong eschatological reference that the motifs of eating bread and the social meal have in the New Testament. Bread is a sign and representation of the coming kingdom of God. "Blessed is he who shall eat bread in the kingdom of God" (Luke 14:15). The second important emphasis is the Johannine equation of bread with the Word, and, indeed, with the person of Jesus: "I am the bread of life; he who comes to me shall not hunger, and he who believes in me shall never thirst" (John 6:35).

An essential theological point is that the two main motifs are not to be seen as alternatives. The main objection to the spiritualizing interpretation is not that it points to the spiritual connections of the concept of bread but that it suppresses the material aspects of the language of Jesus and of the Old Testament in favor of a more or less spiritual understanding. In reality we must take both into account. We must accept the unattenuated material basis but relate it inseparably to the heavenly superstructure, yet not taking these terms in a Marxist sense, which would imply the dependence of heaven on earth, but focusing on the historical core from an eschatological angle.

This is why the Kralitz Bible, the classical Czech translation by the Bohemian Brethren in the sixteenth century, in its note on this text adopted the view of Luther's Small Catechism with its orientation to bodily needs, but made a vital addition, pointing out that what is at issue in "daily bread" is nourishment to sustain soul as well as body. Thus before the fine list of Luther (food, drink, clothes, shoes, houses, farms . . . devout and faithful overlords, good government, etc.), which in part it took over literally, it placed the pure Word of God, faithful preachers, and the sacraments that Christ instituted. The Kralitz Brethren were right. Needs of both body and soul have a place in the unitary New Testament understanding of bread and humanity.

We find this total view in the conduct of Jesus himself. As Joachim Jeremias said:

> The bread which he proffered when he sat at table with publicans and sinners was everyday bread, and yet it was more: the bread of life. . . Every meal his disciples had with him was a usual eating and drinking, and yet it was more: a meal of salvation, a messianic meal, image and anticipation of the meal at the consummation, because he was the master of the house. This remained true in the primitive church: their daily fellowship meals were the customary meals for sustenance, and yet at the same time they were a "Lord's supper" (1 Cor. 11.20) which mediated fellowship with him and linked in fellowship with one another those sitting at table.[15]

Nowhere do we see these two layers or aspects of bread, and of the petition for bread, so clearly and with such powerful implications as in relation to the Last Supper. As Jeremias pointed out, the bread that Jesus broke for the disciples was earthly bread yet also more; it was his body given up to death for many, participation in the atoning power of his death (loc. cit.), an anticipation of feasting in the kingdom of God. This is the starting point of the spiritualizing trend in interpreting the fourth petition of the Lord's Prayer. Its development has often been one-sided. Note the following remarks of Ambrose: "I tell you that before speaking the words of Christ what is offered is called bread, but after speaking them we do not call it bread but body. Why do we say 'our bread' in the Lord's Prayer? We say 'bread,' but *epiousios*, i.e., 'essential' *(supersubstantialis)*. This is

15. Jeremias, *Prayers of Jesus,* pp. 101-2.

not the bread that enters the body but the bread of eternal life which strengthens the essence of the soul."[16]

From a biblical perspective this is a too heavily spiritual understanding. Yet the church's sacramental thinking has had other possibilities. The church never totally lost sight of the unitary understanding of bread. A cause for reflection is that in church history we find a decided orientation to the eucharist particularly in socially alert movements. I have the Hussites especially in mind. Their struggle for the eucharist, and specifically for the granting of Christ's cup to all believers, went hand in hand with a struggle for a more just order in church and society. I think also of the modern ecumenical movement. Influenced especially by the growing presence of Eastern Orthodox theologians with their stress on the eucharist as the inner but outward-radiating center of the Christian life, the ecumenical world has a concern to bring together the spiritual and the social dimensions of the question of bread. In this regard the Russian Orthodox theologian Vitaly Borovoy made a programmatic statement in his rousing address to the Sixth Assembly of the World Council of Churches at Vancouver in 1983: "If the bread of the eucharist is the bread of eternal life and in breaking it we enter into communion with Christ and each other, it is only natural that we should fight against hunger, poverty, illnesses, and other manifestations of social injustices with regard to other people, who are all brothers and sisters."[17]

We must develop these emphases from the eucharistic legacy in expounding and applying the petition for daily bread. Another note that sounds out unmistakably in the term "eucharist," that of thanksgiving, is also very important if we are not to perish of bread alone, or of the struggle for it. Our specifically Christian and essentially human contribution today might

16. Ambrose, *On the Sacraments* V, 4, 24-25; cf. J. Carmignac, *Recherches sur le "Notre Père,"* p. 147; Carmignac gives several other examples of both the spiritualizing and the earthly, bodily interpretation.

17. In David Gill, ed., *Gathered for Life: Official Report, VI Assembly, World Council of Churches* (Geneva: World Council of Churches; Grand Rapids: Eerdmans, 1983), p. 26.

well lie in bearing witness to this dimension. In an article dealing with Swiss relief work, Dietrich Wiederkehr wrote that
various futurists have frightened us with the shock of mutual
destruction and starvation, otherwise we would not be awake.
Yet such forecasts might petrify us as a snake does a mouse. We
might focus nervously only on what we have and what we can
secure for ourselves. Around Jesus, however, another future
may be seen, a vision of people who lead one another out into
the sun, who share bread with one another, who pass a drink of
fresh water from hand to hand. The church can be the fellowship in which this exchange, this mutual enriching and encouraging, is already taking place, in which all find their salvation and their own names in the name of the Lord.[18] The daily
prayer: "Give us this day our daily bread," can and should be a
daily step in this direction.

A note in closing. I began this chapter by quoting Lohmeyer's dictum that the fourth petition is the heart and center
of the Lord's Prayer. I first supported this thesis only with
grammatical considerations, with the shift of perspective that
we see in the text of the prayer at this point. But at the end of
these deliberations we might confirm the statement materially
and theologically as well. We will turn again to Lohmeyer, who
says at the close of his own discussion:

> We can now also understand the position which the peti-
> tion occupies in the Lord's Prayer as a whole. It stands between
> the first three petitions, which are concerned with God, and the
> last three, which are concerned with man; it asks particularly for
> bread, which is given in a special way by God to man. So it is the
> threshold leading from the kingdom of the longed-for eschato-
> logical consummation to the kingdom of present human need,
> and therefore belongs to both kingdoms. At the same time it also
> speaks of the historical and eschatological justification for "our"
> praying for God's name, kingdom and will, for "our" trusting
> him in debt, temptation and evil, and for "our" being the children
> of "Our Father who art in heaven." On the other hand, the peti-

18. Dietrich Wiederkehr, "Solidarischer leben," *Reformatio* 26/3 (1977) 151.

tion for this present and future bread is also an expression of the communion from which we pray to God.[19]

In this sense the fourth petition is indeed the heart and center of the Lord's Prayer.

19. Lohmeyer, *"Lord's Prayer,"* p. 157.

And Forgive Us Our Debts, as We Forgive Our Debtors

Repressed Guilt and Yearning for Identity

At this point in the text the little conjunction "and" appears for the first time. Since this can hardly be accidental, we must not overlook it. The striking "and" is obviously giving us a vital hint. Human need is many-faceted. We must not reduce it to a single aspect, no matter how urgent. Jesus begins with bread in a biblically holy materialism. But a biblically holy materialism cannot stop at the question of bread. We are exposed to other needs in our human living and dying. The truly central need— along with that of daily bread—is the need posed by daily debt or guilt.

Again and again commentators on the Lord's Prayer have rightly devoted thought to the close linking of this petition with the previous one and sought reasons for it. For example, Rudolf Bohren says that the petition for forgiveness belongs to the petition for bread. As truly as we need bread, daily bread, we need forgiveness. As truly as we perish bodily if we have no bread, we perish in soul and also in body if we do not have forgiveness. Bread is no good if forgiveness is not included. Forgiveness is necessary because we never have bread without guilt.[1]

The last sentence might puzzle most of us, and it is hardly tenable as a general statement. But with it Bohren is pointing in a direction that deserves notice. Much more often than we think, we eat daily bread and struggle for it at the expense of others as members of a privileged group in our own society and a privileged nation in world society. We are thus entangled in a nexus and relationship of guilt even when we are not aware of it and do not want to be aware of it. For good reason we may view Marxist theories of class conflict and value, in their dogmatic form, as tendentious and outdated, but if self-righteously and heedlessly we evade their point, namely, the occasion that they give us to examine our personal and collective position in the matter of bread and hunger, then we exhibit a dangerous spiritual (and also in the long run economic) blindness. The little "and" between the fourth and fifth petitions is a summons to our "good conscience" and poor information; it calls us to conversion. Farewell to innocence—an expression which the black church leader in South Africa, Allan Boesak, used as the title for one of his books—is now due. We pray for this as in one breath we pray: "Give us this day our daily bread, and forgive us our debts."

These two essential needs are not always or by everyone felt to be equally urgent. There are people and epochs for whom the question of guilt is overwhelming. The great tragedies of antiquity and the works of perspicacious writers like Dostoyevski and Kafka bear witness to this. In a small way all of us feel something of it in everyday life. But in the main these are exceptions. Most of us feel the need for bread, and suffer from it, much more acutely than we do the problem of guilt. Perhaps this is connected with our physiological makeup. If we still use such phrases as "bodily need" and "spiritual need," we might go along with the vivid argument of Walter Lüthi: the body, especially the stomach, "has a stronger voice, so to speak, for it

1. Bohren, *Das Unser Vater—heute,* p. 85.

grumbles if it does not get bread; it has been given the warning voice of the watchdog. The soul, however, has a softer voice and therefore often goes unheard. The soul does not grumble; it can only sigh."[2] And only too easily we not only fail to hear the sighing but suppress it.

This is true in general. But it applies in a special sense to the prevailing forms of thought and conduct today. It is always risky to try to present the spirit of an age in general trends and tendencies, but one can hardly doubt that in our modern consciousness and behavior, as distinct from those of the Middle Ages and the Reformation, we have much less sense of guilt and readiness to confess it. The dynamic and in many ways contradictory process of modernity from the Renaissance through humanism and the Enlightenment to the present century displays an obvious tendency to abandon the biblical view of the human condition with its emphasis on the depth and scope of our guilty involvement. Concepts like sin have become unintelligible. They are disparaged, suspected of misanthropy. They are viewed as an erratic block, a prehistorical boulder. People walk by such stumbling blocks. They try to ignore them or to deny their significance. There is only "so-called evil," and in principle we already have a handle on that.

With this kind of preconception the status of guilt changes. At the center of attention is not guilt but the guilt complex, the burden of religious and cultural pressures, of authoritarian education, which, it is argued, aims to inculcate a sense of guilt in us so as to be able to manipulate us into a state of contrition. Supposedly, we need not the remission of guilt but the overcoming of such complexes. If the question of guilt still arises, it is shuffled off if possible. We look around for suitable scapegoats. Remarkably, the typical thinking of the age flees from sin, both the term and the reality, but still finds scapegoats. The most influential philosophies and ideologies do this, and we all do it in daily conduct. Almost always something else is guilty: our great economic and social system, our falsely programmed culture

2. Lüthi, *Lord's Prayer*, p. 49.

and civilization, the "evil empire," which is usually on the other side of the "curtain." Even in our own society parents are guilty of the misconduct of their children, protesting young people are guilty of the decay of traditional orders, men are guilty, women are guilty—in short, others are guilty.

Naturally, these accusations are partially true. The related issues must be critically (and self-critically) analyzed. Naturally, modern criticism of the misanthropic aspects of the church's doctrine of sin is not without foundation. We find in the doctrine elements like delight in accusing, dwelling on human weakness and the depiction of vice, interest in portraying the fate of the damned in hell. The role of theology in the development of a guilt complex must be critically (and self-critically) clarified, and we must help to dismantle the complex theologically by teaching and pastoral care. In this regard there is always much to do in the church. But one thing this kind of work must not mean, namely, a flight from the seriousness of the biblical view of sin. Our guilt—racial guilt and personal guilt—must not be covered over or explained away. We must see and confess guilt as an essential human need—our own need. At any rate, the fifth petition of the Lord's Prayer calls us to do this.

Why? To remind the proud again and again of their misdeeds and misery? to wear down their self-consciousness? to quench or freeze their dreams of self-discovery and emancipation? And all this to deliver them up to the tutelage and heteronomy, the alien determination, of religion? to bind their hands with an alien authority, that of a Father in heaven? We constantly hear such postulates, not merely in the history of modern atheism (Marx, Nietzsche, and Sartre), but outside it as well. Religion, especially with its message of sin, is said to be misanthropic and the enemy of emancipation. If we want to find ourselves we must avoid religious bondage, and this means that we must ignore also and especially the summons to confession of guilt.

I want to contradict such postulates and the related interpretations of the petition for forgiveness of debts. We have to admit that one-sided and distorted emphases in church teaching and practice (such as those mentioned) have provoked these misapprehensions. Nevertheless, the complaints do not do justice to the meaning or aim of the Lord's Prayer. On the contrary, the basic concern of serious critics of religion (even among representatives of the modern humanities), namely, to open up ways to human liberation, is in no sense alien to the petition. In the light of it we can in fact take up constructively the very question that is so urgent today: the question of identity.

The petition for forgiveness of debts offers an unusual perspective within the serious concern to find ways to overcome this problem that now occupies so many psychologists and psychiatrists as well as scholars in the humanities. We have only to note the two emphases bound up with the motif. Forgiveness is obviously the basis of our hope outside us, and debt sharpens our awareness of our own responsibility in face of manifestations of alienation before and behind our doors. But does not this mean that the path to self-discovery is doubly blocked? Do not these emphases imply a certain distancing from the self, whereas for self-discovery a resolute turning to the self is advisable?

In his exposition of the related statement about forgiveness of sins in the Creed, Wolfhart Pannenberg has some helpful thoughts in this regard. He allows that confession of one's own sins involves a distancing from the self. Yet that is only one side of the matter. Confession of sins is always confession to oneself, an expression of the readiness to take responsibility for oneself. Seen thus, a Christian sense of sin need not be an expression of self-negation or hostility to life. On the contrary, one may regard it as an affirmation of life even in face of its perversion. Confession of guilt is thus an act of freedom, for true freedom is responsible freedom. Only by taking responsibility for the self can one be identical with oneself.[3]

I might adduce yet another witness. In his book *Krummes Holz—aufrechter Gang,* Helmut Gollwitzer shows how foolish

---

3. Pannenberg, *Das Glaubensbekenntnis ausgelegt und verantwortet vor den Fragen der Gegenwart* (Hamburg: 1972), p. 175.

and misguided is the common idea that in the biblical stress on guilt and responsibility we are treated like children, and that only liberation from religion opens the way to freedom and leads us to dignity. In opposition to this idea Gollwitzer states that accusation may be a very unpleasant way of recognizing freedom but it is at least a very clear one. The accused person is free, the free person accused. Tightening the screw, he then goes on to refer to a danger in the contemporary spirit. It cannot be contested, he says, that often today the same people who claim that Christianity robs us of our adulthood zealously take the same path by dissolving the self in pure determinations. The very seriousness with which the Bible speaks of sin; sin, judgment, and forgiveness as the central contents of the Christian faith; even the phrase "original sin," which is so often misunderstood—these all show that we are nailed fast to our responsibility and therefore to our freedom, and protect us against self-exoneration on the plea that we are under the tutelage of fate, nature, and society.[4]

A report from the United States illustrates this truth. A man under serious accusation rejected the attempts of his defense counselor to minimize his responsibility for the crime by referring to the pressures he had experienced throughout his life. He felt that this kind of defense would be an affront to his personal dignity even though his lawyer believed that he was acting in his best interests. For it is part of our dignity—and promotes self-discovery—that we are able to accept and admit our own guilt.

These deliberations are helpful, of course, only if they do not impose moral demands on those who are tempted and assailed but are set in the context of the story of Jesus and the forgiveness of sins. Then they will naturally provide liberating impulses. In this regard the social dimension of finding identity is also important, as Pannenberg rightly stresses. The degree of freedom is to be measured by our readiness to know that we are responsible for ourselves and also for the circle around us, for

4. Gollwitzer, *Krummes Holz*, pp. 265-66.

all that takes place or does not take place in it. For as a self a person is not an isolated individual but the member of a society and of the whole race. One achieves identity with oneself not by seeking in others guilt for failings in the circle but by accepting one's own guilt and responsibility.[5] Against the common tendency to ease the difficult path of self-discovery by shifting blame to others—parents, family, society—these suggestions offer a correction that is worth considering.

Understood in this way the petition "Forgive us our debts" is not an act of immature self-laceration but an exercise in the Christian freedom for which we are continually to strive.

The Liberation of Unprofitable Servants

Let us now turn more precisely to the wording of the fifth petition. In comparing the two versions in Matthew and Luke, we note that they differ: Matthew has "debts," Luke "sins." The fact that the continuation in Luke then has "debts" ("for we ourselves forgive every one who is indebted to us," 11:4) seems to show that the version in Matthew is original. For obvious reasons Luke replaces the word "debts," which would not normally be used for "sins" in the Greek world, by the more usual term. The substance remains the same.

Nevertheless, it would be good to engage in a close exegesis of the original word. "Debt" (Heb. *hobah*) was a common term in later Judaism to denote our deficiencies in relation to God. "Later Judaism, which views the relation to God as a legal and business relation, often applies the metaphor of indebtedness to the ethical and legal relation between man and God. Man is in arrears with his good works and thus falls into debt with God."[6] There is an account book in heaven in which human deeds and misdeeds are recorded. The relation between assets and debits

5. Pannenberg, *Glaubensbekenntnis*, p. 176.
6. F. Hauck, *TDNT*, 5:561.

decides our destiny. Along these lines Rabbi Akiba can pray: "Our Father, Our King, according to thy great mercy remit our promissory notes."[7]

Jesus adopts this mode of thinking here and also in the parable of the wicked servant (to which we shall return), in the story of the woman who was a great sinner (Luke 7:36-50), and in the saying about the unprofitable servant (Luke 17:10). But he makes a radical change of both content and orientation. He pushes aside the element of accounting. There can be no question of good deeds compensating for bad ones. We owe to God not achievements but ourselves. Karl Barth clearly formulated this aspect of New Testament teaching when he said: "We are God's debtors. We owe him, not something, whether it be little or much, but, quite simply, our person in its totality; we owe him ourselves, since we are his creatures, sustained and nourished by his goodness."[8]

This radicalizing and personalizing of the understanding of debt in the Gospels carry with them both a bitter implication and a promising presupposition. The implication is alarming. If we owe to God ourselves and not just specific debts, we can never pay what we owe. We can never stride on to his eschatological judgment with a good conscience and uplifted head. Even if we succeed in doing the best we can imagine, we are always debtors and never creditors in relation to God. The parable of the servant who waited at table (Luke 17:7ff.) has a relevance that we cannot miss and applies always to all of us: "So you also, when you have done all that is commanded you, say, 'We are unworthy servants; we have only done what was our duty" (v. 10).

But there is another side to this sober reality. It rests on the presupposition that the final accounting or judgment that we face will not be one of literal and mechanical bookkeeping. The omniscient God is not a computer God but our Creator and Re-

7. Babylonian Talmud, Taanit 25b; quoted in *TDNT*, 5:562.

8. Barth, *Prayer According to the Catechisms of the Reformation*, tr. Sara F. Terrien (Philadelphia: Westminster, 1952), p. 65.

deemer whose declared will—we recall our explanation of the third petition—is not an ambivalent Janus-will which might be either yes or no but the will that seeks salvation for his creatures, the will that in Jesus Christ, as Paul maintains with liberating certainty, says an all-surpassing yes to us. We can look ahead to the last judgment, if not with a good conscience, at least with a good knowledge, and in this sense with uplifted head.[9] For we live and die, not to an anonymous calculator, but to our Father in heaven. It is vitally important that we remember the invocation of the Lord's Prayer when expounding the fifth petition.

The Evangelical Primacy of Reconciliation

This point is deepened and strengthened when we turn to the main motif of the fifth petition, that of forgiveness. Briefly, first, we note the connection. The Lord's Prayer speaks of debts or guilt in the context of forgiveness. This accords with the basic theme of the New Testament. In the center is not an accuser but one who overcomes the guilt. His message is not the unmasking but the forgiving of sins. In keeping with this theme the church referred to sin in the Creed only in the context of remission: "I believe in the forgiveness of sins." This puts the problem of guilt in the only light that is possible for Christian theology, which is not interested in debts as such. Sin is not a separate theme in theology. We may think about it theologically only in this context. It is a theme in the history of salvation, not of perdition. Fascination with sin, delight in proving guilt, interest in unmasking sin—at certain times in history the church's preachers and teachers have displayed such attitudes (not to speak of the practice of penance). They were common in the Middle Ages, in the baroque period, and among many Protestant Orthodox and Pietists. But they put the accent in a very dubious place. The questions of religious critics and scholars in

9. Cf. Heidelberg Catechism, Qu. 52.

the humanities—questions to which we referred earlier—were provoked by things of this kind. Rethinking is needed here. We must maintain that the gospel, the Creed, and the Lord's Prayer deal with sin and guilt only within the message of the forgiveness of sins, or the petition: "Forgive us our debts."

The Greek word for "forgive" *(aphienai)* is a common one, at home in both law and economics. It means "to remit," "to release" from legal and financial obligations and duties, including debts. In the Old Testament it occurs in the legal, the cultic, and above all the theological sphere. "In the theophany in *Ex.* 34.6f., God is already called the one who 'forgives iniquity and transgression and sin'; in the Psalter, the 'forgiveness of sins' belongs so much to God's nature and will that the whole fear of God is based firmly upon it (130.4,7f.). To speak of the goodness of God and of the forgiving God is one and the same thing (25.18)."[10] We find the same stress in Judaism. Lohmeyer notes the sixth petition of the Prayer of Eighteen Benedictions: "Forgive us, our Father, we have sinned against thee. Wash away our misdeeds, remove them from thine eyes, for thy mercy is great."

The New Testament takes up these motifs of the Old Testament and Judaism and unites them centrally with the name and story of Jesus Christ, with his word, his deeds, and his destiny.[11] I have in mind the parables of Jesus. In a striking way many of them play upon the theme of the forgiveness of sins. The gospel within the gospel, the parable of the prodigal son, is a particularly clear example (Luke 15:11-32). But we might also refer to the other two parables in the same chapter, that of the lost sheep and that of the lost coin (vv. 1-10). I might adduce, too, the saying of Jesus about the woman who was a great sinner: "Her sins, which are many, are forgiven, for she loved much" (Luke 7:47).

The acts of Jesus as well as his words continually bring the theme of remission to the center of our attention. His healings are signs of the forgiveness of sins: a point of great contention

10. Lohmeyer, *"Lord's Prayer,"* pp. 165-66.
11. On what follows cf. my work *The Faith We Confess,* pp. 227-28 (to which I will also allude elsewhere in commenting on the fifth petition).

116

which evokes the determined resistance of his enemies (Mark 2:1-12) when he claims that "the Son of man has authority on earth to forgive sins" (2:10). His whole life-style as well as his individual acts points to the supreme significance of forgiveness. In contrast to the pious behavior that was expected of him, it was an alternative life-style. He received sinners; he even entered into table fellowship and life fellowship with them, not in accommodation to their sins, but in mediation of forgiveness, liberating and binding them at one and the same time. There is thus great joy in the circle around him. God is coming to the guilty, not willing that they should die, that they should pay their debts at all costs, but willing a new and liberated life for them. His remission of debts, prefigured in the Old Testament by the year of release (Jubilee), is the dawning of great freedom for his people.

What happened to Jesus at Easter, above all his cross and Passion, does not stand in contradiction to the glad news of forgiveness of sins. These events took up the same message once again, this time from the depths. They showed very clearly that remission of guilt does not make guilt innocuous. The alternative life-style of Jesus has nothing whatever to do with "good-time" permissiveness. Sin has to be taken seriously. It often sheds blood and tears, and it costs blood and tears. Christ's forgiveness of sins is an act of solidarity with sinners, a vicarious offering for them, an act of sacrifice on their behalf. The account between God and us is settled on Good Friday. The new covenant of reconciliation is sealed in his blood. "For while we were yet helpless, at the right time Christ died for the ungodly" (Rom. 5:6). This is how Paul puts it in the chapter in which, looking at Christ and Adam, he reflects on the theme of sin and the remission of guilt as the central theme of salvation history.

We firmly maintain that the essential lines of the gospel in the word, deeds, and destiny of Jesus meet at the focal point of the forgiveness of sins. This fact has theological implications. If according to the sure and certain belief of the Evangelists and apostles the definitive (eschatological) concern of God is manifested in the person and history of Jesus, then God is shown to be by nature a forgiving God. The witticism of Voltaire: "God will pardon me—that's his job," is a dreadful saying. It is dreadful because it professionally deforms the true seriousness of forgiveness, which we can in no way take for granted. Nevertheless, taking the saying against the grain, it does make a true and essential point. For God forgiveness is not one of many different possibilities. He has declared his real will to save. This is the one essential reality. If in defining guilt we earlier said that in the biblical sense it does not refer only to individual faults, or to something within us, but to the heart, to the whole person, we can now say that forgiveness does not relate to a something in God, but to the heart of God, to his whole person. This means, however, that the forgiving of debts is the heart of salvation history, of the history of our salvation. The petition "Forgive us our debts" springs from the deepest need and necessity in our temporal and eternal destiny.

Let us look back. We first considered the little connecting word "and" at the beginning of the petition. In this connection we spoke of the two indissolubly linked needs, bread and forgiveness of debts. We noted that most commentators try to differentiate the two problems, allotting them to the two spheres of human existence, bread to the body and forgiveness to the soul. So long as this is a matter of specific emphasis and not of demarcation, of a rigid division of labor, we have no objection. Nor do we object to the distinction made by Gerhard Ebeling when he tried to stress the more radically existential necessity of the forgiveness of sins: "We must at all events maintain that forgiveness of debts, as distinct from what is necessary in order to live, points to that which is necessary in order to die.... The forgiveness of our debts must prove to be a necessity of existence even more urgent and more radical than the necessity of daily bread. For the latter is not needed for death, but forgiveness of debts is needed in undivided unity for both life and death— needed for life because it is needed for death, needed for death because it is needed for life."[12] This is true as a matter of empha-

12. Ebeling, *On Prayer*, pp. 64-65.

sis and so long as we keep in view the unity of our temporal and eternal destiny both ways. As the time-oriented petition for daily bread also raises the question of the bread of eternal life, so the eschatological will of God to forgive sins finds something among us that corresponds to it even today in time.

Danger Points

This leads us to the next clause in the petition, which must not be overlooked: "And forgive us our debts, as we forgive our debtors." The additional clause is striking in every respect. With regard to form, in the structure of the Lord's Prayer it is the only petition with two members. With regard to context, at the end of the prayer this point is stressed once again: "For if you forgive men their trespasses, your heavenly Father also will forgive you; but if you do not forgive men their trespasses, neither will your Father forgive your trespasses" (Matt. 6:14-15). With regard to consequences, only here is the petition directly related to corresponding practice on the part of those who pray. The matter was obviously very important for the Evangelists and for Jesus himself.

The Old Testament and Apocrypha offer some precedents. Thus we read in Sirach 28:2-4 that we are to forgive any who wrong us, for the Lord will forgive our sins if we ask him, but if we remain unreconciled to others, we cannot expect forgiveness from the Lord. The motif occurs time and again in the Gospels. The only reference to the Lord's Prayer in Mark may be found in this leading motif: "And whenever you stand praying, forgive, if you have anything against any one; so that your Father also who is in heaven may forgive you your trespasses" (Mark 11:25). In the broader compass of the Sermon on the Mount there is again a strong emphasis upon the point, not merely in connection with prayer, but also with making an offering: "So if you are offering your gift at the altar and there remember that your brother has something against you, leave your gift there before the altar and go; first be reconciled to your brother, and then come and offer your gift" (Matt. 5:23-24).

In addition to these weighty references, one might also regard a parable of Jesus as a commentary on the petition for forgiveness: that of the wicked servant (Matt. 18:23-35). The story is impressive and close to life. A powerful king is settling accounts with his subjects. One of them is in debt and insolvent. All his goods and family are to be sold. But when he makes a desperate plea to his master, in sheer mercy the latter remits his debt. His position eased in this way, the forgiven servant, as a creditor, proceeds to settle accounts with his own debtors. Though the amounts owed are very small by comparison, he violently enforces payment. When the lord hears of it, he is hurt and offended by such implacable behavior. He retracts his decision and in holy anger hands the wicked servant over to the torturers. The last verse of the parable presses home the lesson: "So also my heavenly Father will do to every one of you, if you do not forgive your brother from you heart" (v. 35).

Beyond question, forgiveness is not a one-dimensional matter, a one-way street. When we ask it of God and receive it from him, it sets us in motion toward others. It calls for personal and social responses. How are we to understand this? We must avoid a possible misunderstanding of the indissoluble connection. It is not as if our readiness to forgive triggered God's forgiveness; as if our own act of forgiveness preceded, though not taking precedence over, God's act of reconciliation; as if this act of ours were a precondition for the bringing into force of God's will to save. There have actually been interpretations of this kind in church history, and there are still some (perhaps unwittingly) today.

Let me give an illustration from the history of dogma. The fifth petition of the Lord's Prayer played an important part in the church's debates about Pelagianism. In 416 the bishops at the second council of Milevis (Augustine among them) wrote to Pope Innocent to draw his attention to a new heresy which devalued the grace of Christ and even tried to detach the Lord's Prayer from the church and the orthodox understanding, claiming that it is possible to reach such a state of perfection in the Christian life that there is no longer any need to pray the fifth petition. In 518 the sixteenth council of Carthage stated accordingly that those who say that the saints no longer need use the words "Forgive us our debts," since they no longer need pray this on their own behalf but only for the sinners among their peoples, let them be anathema.[13]

The criticism adopted by the bishops' council was fundamentally right. True, the heretics were standing for a valid emphasis. In this petition Christians do not think only of themselves but of the sin of the world. They pray it in solidarity with the whole race that is entangled in guilt. What we said elsewhere about the open "we" of the Lord's Prayer (the fellowship of believers, not insulated from the world, but turning toward it) must be remembered at this point. This does not mean, however, that the request for forgiveness is for export only. In solidarity with the world, Christians are aware of their own debts and their own need of forgiveness, always, everywhere, by all. Before God the communion of saints is never a fellowship of creditors but always a fellowship of debtors.

This is a vital point if we are to understand the two parts of the fifth petition. By being ready to forgive and actually forgiving, we do not posit or set up a condition to which divine forgiveness is linked. Our chances of salvation would be poor if they depended on our own good will. God's pardon is not conditional on ours. The worth of our supplication is conditional on our prior pardon.[14] The point of the second clause is precisely the sincerity, or, better, the credibility of our praying and living. Werner Pfendsack commands our assent when he writes that the fifth petition of the Lord's Prayer is the most dangerous petition of the whole prayer. In none other does the danger lurk so close that praying we lie, and lying we pray.[15]

In the direct context of the Lord's Prayer the whole of Mat-

---

13. Cf. J. Carmignac, *Recherches sur le "Notre Père,"* p. 233.
14. Ibid., p. 231.
15. Pfendsack, *Unser Vater,* p. 69.

thew 6 warns us against the danger of pious lying. The fifth petition fights against the devout schizophrenia of those who pray
to God for forgiveness but refuse forgiveness to others. The need
and necessity of remitting debts is indivisible. The movement
from God to us and from us to our contemporaries must be an
unbroken one. Forgiveness cannot stop with us. We cannot mo-
nopolize it. We must pass it on to others. In intercession and
practice we must declare and transmit it to them. To refuse forgiveness to others, whether near or distant, is no less than to
maneuver oneself out of the life-giving power of the forgiveness
of debts by Jesus. It is here in the forgiveness and reconciliation
that we do not and must not refuse that the credibility of our
Christian life is decided.

Furthermore, what is at issue here is an essential service
that we can render to the redeeming and healing of relationships
in our human world. Is it not true that one of the most threatening and destructive problems in human history is bound up
with the problem of guilt and forgiveness, or, specifically, with
the assigning of guilt and the refusing of forgiveness? The most
devilish of vicious circles are found precisely here, and they have
that tendency to accelerate or escalate which is typical in the
matter of counting debts. I recall a short story by L. N. Tolstoy
about the neighbors Ivan and Gavrilo in a Russian village. For
many years they lived in neighborly peace. But suddenly a quar-
rel arose and the unhappy spiral of misunderstandings and accusations mounted up fatally. It began with a misplaced hen's
egg, continued with angry words on the part of the women and
children and scufflings on that of the men, and finally half the
village fell victim to the flames. Only then did the word of forgiveness and reconciliation come, and with it reconstruction.

Thus it is again and again in human life on the small personal scale. Nor do things differ in the larger world of politics.
If there is not hot war there is cold war. Others are said to be
guilty; accounts are settled. Nations arm against one another.
Armaments escalate. This has always been so in history, but in
our own day, with the inconceivably enhanced potential for destruction, it has reached the height of madness. Misleading

terms are used, but the deadly spiral goes on in both the personal sphere and the political.

The Bible looks very realistically at this fatal tendency in the human heart and human history, and contradicts it. We have only to look at its first chapters. Sin escalates alarmingly in the stories of the beginnings of the race from the Fall to fratricide and then the Flood. It is very vividly depicted. And the divine command constantly seeks to dam up the flow. This is the point of the Mosaic "eye for an eye and tooth for a tooth" (Exod. 21:24). We misunderstand this principle if we see in it a divine concession to barbaric customs. It is meant to put a brake on the temptation to escalate the settling of debts. Thus far: "An eye for an eye and a tooth for a tooth," but no further.

In the New Testament Jesus probes more deeply. He sets against this command of Moses his own radicalized command: "But I say unto you, Do not resist one who is evil. But if any one strikes you on the right cheek, turn to him the other also" (Matt. 5:39). This is to tackle temptation at the root, which is the refusal of forgiveness. We have not just to put the brake on here. We have to take the offensive against that refusal in the strategy of love.

The petition must be construed in this radical context of the Sermon on the Mount. It appeals to the divine forgiveness and presses for the passing on of this forgiveness in our guilt-laden human world. Is this pure idealism? No, it is our chance for life and survival. At any rate it begins very concretely with the praying person and the praying society. It does not promote an idealistic ideology of prayer and forgiveness. *Orare et laborare*, to pray *and* to work, means that sober analyses of the mechanism of guilt and sober pastoral and social initiatives against them are part of praying. The Christian witness to forgiveness does not mean viewing guilt as innocuous, wiping out antitheses, or suppressing conflicts. To master guilt, whether in the private sphere or the public sphere, does not mean sweeping things under the rug, whether a private rug or a public rug. We can and must settle conflicts.

But we can and must settle them on the basis of forgiveness and with a view to it. We cannot forget, but we can forgive. The petition advocates the possibility of a new beginning between both individuals and nations. It should not be provisionally suspended in the sharpness of tension or the heat of battle. Here lies the chance and contribution of the Christian community in situations of conflict. Persistent concern for a new beginning even with those on the other side of this or that barricade is part of the actuality and power of the petition: "Forgive us our debts, as we forgive our debtors."

To show what encouragement this view of things can give on the political scene, I will turn to a German theologian and politically very alert contemporary, Hans-Joachim Iwand. In the difficult postwar years, laden with guilt and hatred, Iwand worked steadfastly to bridge the dreadful gulf between the European nations East and West. He depicts as follows a meeting with the Czech theologian J. L. Hromádka in the course of his efforts.

> It was more than one of the usual meetings . . . We were certain that nothing and no one could remedy what had happened . . . One thing alone could be said: Our very great fault. The primary thing in guilt is not who is guilty. Many people examine the historical facts like prosecutors trying to determine who is guilty and who is not. But the situation is different with guilt in the historical sense, the irreparable sense. Here it is a matter of assuming it. It is the narrow gate through which the way lies ahead. In and for itself it is like a stone in the path. No one wants to pick it up. No one wants to carry it. All who are not caught in the act steer clear of it. In this way we run away from our own history and escape from the visitations and the promise of God. . . . Something happened here that we have to master if history, European history, is to go on and not to be condemned to futile decay. . . . At the heart of our first conversation was guilt, the mastering of guilt, and our brotherhood, which offered itself to us on that evening as a gift that was ready for us long before we knew one another or had that meeting.[16]

16. Iwand, "Der Brief zum 70. Geburtstag von J. L. Hromádka," *Communio viatorum* (1959) 126-27.

And Lead Us Not into Temptation

Tempted Left and Right

Martin Luther is reputed to have said that he went to bed with the fifth petition and woke up with the sixth.[1] This saying admirably characterizes the human situation as Luther saw it. At the end of each segment of life we are debtors, and the petition "Forgive us our debts" is the petition that we need as we look at our balance sheet. "We are beggars, that is true," was very logically the last of Luther's reported sayings. Yet there is no less need, as we begin each new day, to pray: "And lead us not into temptation." For each and every day our whole life is exposed to temptation and assault.

Few people have had this experience, or thought about it, more deeply than the German Reformer. Temptation is one of the key words in his life and theology. "Temptation makes a theologian"—of whom can this be said more justifiably than of Luther? This is not to make temptation innocuous, let alone to glorify it. It has in fact been glorified in the history of ethical thinking and in everyday conduct. It has been welcomed as a challenge, as a chance to prove oneself, as a test in the develop-

---

1. A. Köberle, *Das Vaterunser und der Mensch in der Gegenwart* (Stuttgart: 1940), p. 14.

ment of one's powers. "What does not do away with me makes me stronger"—a Nietzsche can say this, but not a Luther. The sixth petition does not accord with the spirituality of a modern heroism of that type. It does not run: "Lead us into temptation," but: "Lead us not into temptation." We must not fail to note this first negative in the Lord's Prayer. We may not say that temptation is welcome. We certainly must not provoke it. If possible, we must avoid it. It is as big a threat to us as fire, and one does not play with fire.

What was the setting of the sixth petition for Luther? In his "Exposition of the Lord's Prayer for Simple Laymen, 1519," he offers an impressive account. Temptation is a universal and many-faceted phenomenon. We cannot localize it or limit it to specific situations. It is omnipresent in our human world. We are beset by it behind and before and cannot steer clear of it (p. 73). It threatens us left and right (an allusion to Ps. 91:7: "A thousand may fall at your [left] side, ten thousand at your right hand"), and this distinction provides an occasion for Luther to speak about that two basic types of temptation (as was customary; cf. also Calvin and Amandus Polanus).

Temptation threatens on the left hand in situations of weakness. By these Luther means sickness, poverty, dishonor, and anything that injures us, especially when our will, plan, opinion, counsel, word, or work is rejected and despised. We are then incited to anger, hatred, bitterness, and impatience. This is humanly understandable, but to fall into this temptation is a snare. In particular, two overhasty conclusions seem obvious. In difficult circumstances some harden their hearts and defy God. Others, pointing to the power of temptation, say that they are impotent victims and take no responsibility. Luther protests that we are never totally helpless when we come under the burden of circumstances. And he offers a parable from a favorite medieval book: You cannot stop a bird flying in the air but you can stop it building a nest in your hair (p. 75). This means that we cannot help being exposed to temptations but we need not give in to them; we can resist them. The invoking of God that we find in the sixth petition is an effective weapon in this spiritual battle.

What about temptation on the right hand? We are to think here of a position of strength. The person tempted is in a privileged situation, is doing well in life, and gets on with others. Everything seems to be in order, but this very situation brings with it more dangerous temptation than a position of weakness. Luther alludes here to the saying already quoted from Psalm 91. If a thousand fall on the left side, ten thousand fall on the right. For those on the right hand are tempted into licentiousness, debauchery, arrogance, avarice, and vainglory. These are the snares of success. In his own day Luther found the greatest danger on the right hand. He bewailed the relationships and modes of conduct of his contemporaries, with a specially sharp eye for young people. The world was seeking goods, fame, and sensual pleasure. The young especially were no longer learning soon enough how to combat carnal lust and temptation. They were falling victim to them so that without any shame the whole world was now full of stories and songs of whoredom and wantonness as though this were a good thing. Luther realized that it was a severe temptation for the young when the devil blew into their flesh and kindled bone and marrow and members, also enticing them from without with sights and gestures, dances, clothes, words, and attractive male and female images. As Job said, "his breath kindles coals" (41:21). So the whole world madly offers its enticements with clothes and ornaments (p. 76).

Faced with such philippics, whether smirking or sighing, we can only ask what Luther would have to say about behavior in our age. We might, of course, put the critical counterquestion whether in this analysis of the temptations of his day the primary focus is not on the conduct of young people and on sexual (im)morality. This seems to be typical of critics of culture and morals in every age, including our own. It involves a foreshortening of the problem of temptation. Undoubtedly, Luther's train of thought shows this bias. Yet we should not overlook the fact that this is not the Reformer's total view but the climax of his exposition. He thinks it important to state that temptation covers all human life. It besets us left and right, behind and before. It calls us into question on every hand. The point is that we must note soberly and take seriously this threat to our lives, and especially that we must not yield to it. We must not go with the tempting trends of the age but resist them, praying: "Lead us not into temptation." This opens up some of the biblical motifs regarding temptation to which we shall now turn in detail.

The History of Temptation with God

Temptation is a leading theme in the biblical message. It runs like a red thread through biblical history. As Lohmeyer said,

> We might call the Bible, the Old and New Testaments, the "Book of Temptations". On its first pages stands the temptation of the first man and woman, and on its last the prophetic descriptions of the great temptation which is "coming on the whole world, to try those who dwell on the earth" (*Rev.* 3.10). Between this beginning and this end there stretches the history of the people of God and with it the histories of individual men of God, and this single history, too, is a continuous chain of temptations which begins with Abraham and does not end with Jesus and his disciples; indeed, to speak of a divine history means to speak of the continuous series of temptations which has gone on since the world was created and will go on until it ends.[2]

This very significant theme, this dramatic history, is developed in the biblical witness in many different ways. We can distinguish various motifs. It is not easy, nor would it be permissible, to reduce them to a common denominator. I want to point out four aspects of the theme of temptation (Greek *peirasmos*), trying to get close to the meaning of the sixth petition in four different ways. The steps will gradually bring us nearer to the central biblical understanding of temptation.

We will begin with the type in which, in relation to God, we are not objects of temptation but subjects. God does not

2. Lohmeyer, *"Lord's Prayer,"* p. 198.

tempt us; we tempt God. Both the Old Testament and the New know this situation. The classic example is in Exodus, in the contest of the story of the exodus. The liberated people murmur against their liberator because they do not have enough water to drink. For the sake of the water jugs and fleshpots of Egypt they are on the point of despising the freedom they have been given. "Why did you bring us up out of Egypt?" (17:3). Moses says that this grumbling and murmuring is a tempting of Yahweh: "Why do you tempt the Lord?" (v. 2). He calls the place Massah and Meribah because of the people's tempting and faultfinding. I would call this a temptation on the left hand. We have an understandable if shortsighted and ungrateful human reaction in an hour of great need. The people no longer cling to the promises but look only at circumstances, despising their freedom and tempting God—something that God's people are often inclined to do.

The New Testament contains a vivid story that we might call an example of temptation on the right hand. It is the story of Ananias and Sapphira in Acts 5. It occurs in connection with the account of the apostolic "communism of love." The first Christians formed a brotherly and sisterly fellowship to which individuals and families brought their goods to help the needy. They did so voluntarily; no one was compelled. Ananias and Sapphira wanted to have a part, but halfheartedly. They did not say that they were laying only a part of the goods that they had sold at the apostles' feet, and even worse, when asked directly, one after the other they bore false witness. This halfhearted tactic, this mock-holy playing with God and the community, Peter called a tempting of God, or, even more pointedly, a tempting of the Spirit of the Lord (Acts 5:9). It thus came close to the sin against the Holy Spirit, the one sin for which the New Testament says there is no forgiveness. One neither can nor should play games with God or try to deceive him. "It is a fearful thing to fall into the hands of the living God" (Heb. 10:31).

Scripture speaks much more often about God's testing of us than of our tempting of God, and first, in what is a surprising way after what has just been said, in a very confident and positive sense. In the biblical use of *peirasmos* we certainly catch the note of threat but also the motif of opportunity. *Peirasmos* has two emphases and many languages have two words for it: Latin *tentatio* and *probatio,* English *temptation* and *test,* French *tentation* and *épreuve,* German *Versuchung* and *Prüfung,* Czech *pokušení* and *zkouška.* In all these languages and in the Greek *peirasmos* the two aspects are very closely related but they need to be differentiated according to use and situation. In the present context the biblical term has the sense of trying, testing, or proving.

Biblical piety does not view this element negatively, especially in the Old Testament. On the contrary, the Bible sees testing as part of the life of faith. Faith in the biblical sense is not a path that is guaranteed and secure. It is a living by promises, not by circumstances. The confrontation with circumstances brings temptations, as we have just seen. But we must not fear these or try to evade them for fear of failure. We must see them as opportunities to prove faith. They are challenges in which faith is tested and purified. Biblical salvation history is precisely a history of temptation in this sense. It involves risk and many dangers, but it is also full of promise.

A good example may be found in Abraham, the father of faith, whose obedience underwent a bitter test when God commanded him to offer up his son Isaac (Gen. 22:1-19). One might also think of other patriarchs and prophets: Jacob and his battle of faith, David and his many temptations. Above all we think of the story of Job, whose faithfulness to God is put to an intolerable test, who is tempted on the left hand, and who does not keep silence but utters the violent protest of assaulted faith, appealing from God to God. The seriousness of his pious remark: "Shall we receive good at the hand of God, and shall we not receive evil?" was severely tested. In this sense biblical temptation is the moment of truth.

Biblical faith has a profound interest in this truth, in its objective and subjective demonstration, in the proving of its integrity. Hence the biblical witnesses can even ask God to test them. This fact is unforgettably expressed in Ps. 139, which extols

God's all-encompassing nearness in the midst of life, but closes with the words of prayer: "Search me, O God, and know my heart! Try me, and know my thoughts! And see if there be any wicked way in me, and lead me in the way everlasting!" (vv. 23-24). (Another rendering is: "And see if there be any hurtful way in me, and lead me in a straight way.") Clarifying the inner and outer ambiguities that assail all of us all our lives—"I believe, Lord, help my unbelief" (Mark 9:24)—was a profound concern of the people of the Bible. They thus asked God for this clarification even at the cost of a by no means pleasant trial, confident that such a trial would not finally be a divine cat-and-mouse game but that God's concern no less than theirs was the proving and preserving of faith, not its weakening but its strengthening: "I believe, Lord, *help* my unbelief."

This view of temptation is particularly clear and close to home in the apocryphal book of Judith. The people of Israel were put to a hard test when confronted by the overwhelming power of the Assyrians under Holofernes. In face of this test Judith made to the leading men of Bethulia the clarifying and encouraging statement that in it all they must think of the Lord their God, who was testing them as he had tested their forefathers. They were to remember his dealings with Abraham, his testing of Isaac, and the experiences of Jacob when he fed the flock of his uncle Laban in Mesopotamia. God put them all through the fire in order to see whether they would hold fast to him. He did not now have punishment and destruction in mind but was disciplining them as friends so that they might know him better (8:24ff.). This passage undoubtedly views God's testing, not as the act of an enemy, as crushing punishment, but as the act of a friend, as an opportunity for purification. Nor should we overlook the fact that what follows this interpretation is the exemplary initiative of Judith in prayer and action. We must seize the opportunity.

In the New Testament this view of temptation seems to retreat somewhat into the background. Yet it is not wholly absent. The main thrust of apostolic exhortation is that the brothers and sisters should master and grasp as opportunities the assaults to which the Christian churches were exposed from the very first. Thus Paul wrote to Corinth, the church with which he had to wrestle most in regard to various problems and temptations, that its members must not capitulate to assaults or yield to temptations. We are not defenseless against them. There is no reason fatalistically to make peace with them. Christians, of course, must have no illusions as to the peril. "Let any one who thinks that he stands take heed lest he fall." Yet a confident promise follows this sober warning. "No temptation has overtaken you that is not common to man. God is faithful, and he will not let you be tempted beyond your strength, but with the temptation will also provide the way of escape, that you may be able to endure it" (1 Cor. 10:12-13).

The New Testament regards the opportunity that temptation offers primarily as an opportunity to demonstrate and clarify faith. 1 Peter is especially impressive on this point when it uses the illustration of gold tested in the fire. When proved in the same way, faith, the imperishable and unadulterated inheritance of Christians, is found to be more precious than perishable gold (1:6-7). If we remember this, then although temptation will undoubtedly cause us much distress at the time, we can still welcome it with hope as an instrument of purification: "Count it all joy, my brethren, when you meet various trials, for you know that the testing of your faith produces steadfastness" (Jas. 1:2-3). In the apostolic witness regarding the temptations of everyday Christian life, the note of sober, patient confidence is not lacking: "Blessed is the man who endures trial, for when he has stood the test he will receive the crown of life" (1:12).

Tempted by Others

More dangerous and common is the third type of temptation that we find in the Bible and human life, that is, tempting by others. We recall Luther's description. Largely, though not exclusively, everyday temptation takes place within the human sphere. It has to do with our social life. Co-humanity is the basic biblical category in the understanding of humanity. I am a Thou to others. I am a social being. There is no real or true humanity apart from my relations with others, with God and with those alongside me. Here again we must pay attention to the invocation of the Lord's Prayer. It ties us to our brothers and sisters before God. I am not alone before God when I pray. God is *our* Father.

Here lies humanity's richness and opportunity. But although that is true, after the Fall here lies also the threat and peril. We must take the words "after the Fall" in a strict sense. The story of the Fall, we remember, is a story of temptation (Gen. 3). Hence we must not overlook the striking figure of the serpent, and from a wider angle we must devote attention to this figure. Nevertheless, it is beyond question that we are tempted and enticed by others. The dialogs in the story are important in this regard. We stand or fall in our relation to the Thou. On the serpent's initiative Adam is tempted by Eve. This bears no relation to an allocation of roles, as exposition has only too often supposed to the detriment of women. The Bible is well aware of the reciprocity of temptation by others. True, women do tempt men. We need think only of Potiphar's wife in the story of Joseph (Gen. 39:7ff.). But no less common and often even more dangerous is the other form of temptation, as the Old Testament especially depicts it; men tempt, seduce, and force women, not only rough men (as in the story of Tamar in 2 Sam. 13), but the elect of God (as in that of David and Bathsheba in 2 Sam. 11). The Bible does not allot roles in this regard. It simply states that mutually and in many different ways we become snares to one another.

This is true not only in the relation between men and women. Other spheres as well as the sexual can become spheres of enticement and temptation. Even and especially the religious sphere: How impressively and with what is for us almost unimaginable strictness the prophets and apostles warn against alien cults and enticements to apostasy from the faith of God's people! In the sphere of ethics and morals, too, they warn against being influenced by an alien life-style that is contrary to the divine commands. Proverbs offers an impressive depiction of this temptation: "My son, if sinners entice you, do not consent. If they say, 'Come with us, let us lie in wait for blood, let us wantonly ambush the innocent . . . we shall find all precious goods, we shall fill our houses with spoil; throw in your lot among us, we will all have one purse' —my son, do not walk in the way with them, hold back your foot from their paths" (1:10-15).

In an alienated world that is characterized by sin, temptation can take a structural form and even become the basic law of everyday life. The New Testament often speaks of "this world" along these lines as the power of temptation to which Christians are continually exposed in their attempts to live the Christian life. Thus Paul can open one of the weightiest ethical passages in his Epistles with the admonition: "Do not be conformed to this world, but be transformed by the renewal of your mind, that you may prove what is the will of God" (Rom. 12:2). In my view we are not just to take the term "this world" timelessly. The fashion of this world changes, and so do its temptations, taking various cultural forms. Hence the admonition not to conform ourselves is also formulated as a summons to prove, that is, soberly to analyze the phenomena of temptation. We must constantly work out Christian ethics and discipleship afresh in relation to the morality of the time.

In this respect we can learn much from alien voices. I am impressed today by the analyses in which the young Marx found a system of (capitalist) temptation in the society of his day. His formulations are drastic and possibly exaggerated, but unfortunately they are close enough to life. "A eunuch does not flatter his base master, or seek by more infamous means to increase his diminished usefulness so as surreptitiously to obtain a favor in the way that the industrial eunuch, the producer, does to get some silver pennies, to entice money from the pocket of his beloved Christian neighbor. . . . Every product is a bait to attract the other's essence, his money, to oneself, and every real or possible need is a weakness to lead the bird into the trap."[3]

Questions such as these, which arise, mutatis mutandis, in the spheres of power politics, culture, and fashion as well as economics, need to be put again and again. Why is it that we today come so strongly under the seductive pressure of the mass media as they are exploited in the interests of power and profit? Where are the particularly dangerous manipulators at work with their hidden and insidious temptations? At what point are we especially vulnerable? Where must we warn, and against what must we protest and fight? These questions, too, undoubtedly belong to the sphere in which the petition applies: "Lead us not into temptation."

Satanic Testing

The New Testament pays more attention to the fourth aspect of the *peirasmos* motif than to those that we have discussed thus far. One might call this the deepest layer of the whole problem and the one that brings us much closer to an understanding of the petition "And lead us not into temptation." It concerns the last, great, eschatological temptation. There are penultimate, provisional temptations, everyday tests such as we all know. But the Bible also speaks of an ultimate testing, and it does so especially in apocalyptic sections. I have in mind, for example, the Synoptic apocalypse in Mark 13 (and par.). This passage depicts in somber hues the threatened end-time of the world, a crisis without parallel: "For in those days there will be such tribulation as has not been from the beginning of the creation which God created until now, and never will be" (v. 19). It will be a time of apostasy and betrayal: "Brother will deliver up brother to

---

3. K. Marx and F. Engels, *Kleine ökonomische Schriften* (Berlin: Dietz, 1955), p. 141; cf. my book *Encountering Marx: Bonds and Barriers Between Christians and Marxists*, tr. Edwin H. Robinson (Philadelphia: Fortress, 1977), pp. 58ff.

death, and the father his child, and children will rise up against parents and have them put to death" (v. 12). A special feature of such days will be that they are days of temptation in the special sense that false messiahs and prophets will arise to lead Christians astray (v. 22).

The book of Revelation portrays the time of temptation with alarming vividness. It is "the hour of trial which is coming on the whole world, to try those who dwell upon the earth" (3:10). It is a temptation of ecumenical and indeed cosmic scope. "*Peirasmos* here is not so much the temptation of the individual; it is rather the total eschatological terror and tribulation of the last time."[4] But individuals suffer too. Decision is here made concerning all of us, concerning our final salvation or perdition. We can in some sense win many battles in the fight against everyday temptations and lose the last battle. We can also lose many fights with penultimate temptations and gain life in the last struggle. This is the final test, the last judgment.

A difference from the trials to which we have referred already, however, is that our chances of mastering this final temptation are minimal and even nonexistent if we are counting on our own powers. All that we can do here is pray: "Lead us not into [this] temptation." Why? The apostle gives the answer in a familiar passage in Ephesians: "We are not contending against flesh and blood, but against the principalities, against the powers, against the world rulers of this present darkness, against the spiritual hosts of wickedness in the heavenly places" (6:12). Undoubtedly, this passage is heavily mythological. The apostle does not hesitate to use the demonic categories of the imaginings and thinking of the prevailing worldviews of his day. We have good reason, and we are right, to demythologize his world of ideas. The work of clarification done by the Enlightenment must be largely respected. Yet this work definitely went too far when in discarding demonological notions it was also prepared to abandon the biblical core of the apostolic message that these notions were meant to express, namely, the point that in our world that

4. H. Seesemann, *TDNT*, 6:30.

is characterized by the Fall and sin we are not dealing only with flesh and blood, with natural weakness, but with principalities and powers, with a revolt against God, with the concentrated force of evil that our good intentions cannot match. Any enlightenment that misses this point falls short. We need a second and more realistic enlightenment such as will be intelligible to us in the twentieth century after the Holocaust and face to face with the inconceivable possibility of planetary and cosmic disruption. This dimension is part of what the Bible has in view when it speaks about temptation.

We must not overlook the fact that at key places in the biblical accounts of temptation there appears the sinister figure of the tempter or accuser, Satan. Already at the beginning of the Bible, in the story of the Fall, his ambivalent contours may be seen in the puzzling form of the serpent. Satan is then named in the prologue to Job. He is the driving force behind the torments to which the pious Job, with the consent and under the final control of God, is subjected. In the Gospels he is a serious opponent in connection with the coming of Jesus. The apostles see him threateningly and dangerously at work to counteract their mission. On the whole, it is true, Satan appears in the Bible only sporadically. There can be no question here of the kind of dualism that was a strong possibility in the religious history of the time, as in Persian religion or later in Gnosticism. No satanology counterbalances theology or christology. We must respect the sporadic and fragmentary nature of Satan's appearances in our own reflections. It would be a definite mistake to try to make of the theology of the devil and demons an independent theme, or even to "catalogue" it.

On this matter, which is so often misleading and misunderstood, I agree with Karl Barth when he wrote: "Far from me be the idea of preaching the Devil to you. One cannot preach him, and I do not at all intend to cause you anguish. Nevertheless, there is in this matter a reality that we modern Christians pass over too lightly. There exists a superior, ineluctable enemy whom we cannot resist unless God comes to our aid. I do not care for demonology, nor for the manner in which it is treated in Germany today [1947] and perhaps elsewhere. Ask me no questions about the Demon, for I am not an authority on the subject! However, it is necessary for us to know that the Devil exists, but then we must hasten to get away from him."[5]

In fidelity to the biblical view we must keep a sober distance here. Yet we must not confuse this with an ignoring of the problem that tames it. We must recognize and take seriously the depth of our human alienation in its true urgency and of our temptation in its menacing reality. When Peter writes: "Your adversary the devil prowls around like a roaring lion, seeking some one to devour" (1 Pet. 5:8), this is more than poetic, mythological hyperbole. In its own way it is a realistic reference to the seriousness of the situation which strips away all illusions. His unmistakably realistic point lies in the admonition: "Be sober, be watchful." A proverb tells us that the road to hell is paved with good intentions. It is a wise proverb, theologically wise. Good intentions are no doubt attractive and meaningful in everyday life, but we cannot resist satanic temptation with them. Hence the admonition: "Be sober, be watchful."

It seems very important that we should clearly and firmly work out this point which lies behind what the Bible says about satanic temptation. Otherwise a misunderstanding lies in wait, namely, the idea that the reference to Satan and demons diminishes or even suspends our own responsibility in an alienated world. Christians and religious people often fall into this danger. They say that they have had a face-to-face encounter with demons when really they ought to speak about their own failure and confess their own guilt. A strong demonology may become a means of self-exculpation. But the biblical references to Satan, with their call for soberness, do not support this. They do not demobilize us. On the contrary, they mobilize us for resistance. The thrust of the Ephesians text that we quoted above is resistance, not capitulation: "Therefore take the whole armor of God, that you may be able to withstand in the evil day, and having done all, to stand" (6:13). The only point is that it is the

5. Barth, *Prayer*, pp. 73-74.

armor of *God*. On this alone can the sober hope of Christians— a Nevertheless-hope—be solidly established in face of the satanic dimension of temptation. This brings us to the final dimension or aspect of the biblical view of temptation.

The Story of the Temptation

Our perspective on temptation would be definitely too restricted were we to forget that in the biblical witness there is not only our tempting of God and our own tempting by God or Satan but also the temptation of Jesus in our place.

In some sense the whole course of the life of Jesus was a history of temptation. It came to a head in his Passion. We recall Gethsemane, which was clearly a situation of temptation. As we showed expressly in expounding the petition "Thy will be done," it was so as Jesus wrestled with and for the will of the Father: "My soul is very sorrowful, even to death. . . . My Father, if it be possible, let this cup pass from me; nevertheless, not as I will, but as thou wilt" (Matt. 26:38-39). Note then the address to the disciples, which expressly takes up the motif of temptation, empowering them, as it were, to meet the great tests ahead: "Watch and pray that you may not enter into temptation" (v. 41). And then we think of the cry of dereliction on the cross: "My God, my God, why hast thou forsaken me?"—the final and in a true sense eschatological assault. Descending into ultimate God-forsakenness (the Son of God's descent into hell as Calvin understood it), Jesus takes upon himself this truly hellish temptation.

The story of the temptation of Jesus (in the narrower sense) in Matthew 4:1ff. and Luke 4:1ff. offers us an emphatic and impressive depiction. It also gives the temptation a spiritual interpretation (we are to think of the Holy Spirit!). It gives essential material content to the biblical motif of temptation. We must now deal with it briefly.

By no means accidentally the Evangelists Matthew and Luke put the story after the baptism of Jesus and before the commencement of his public work. In baptism Jesus receives, with the Spirit, full authority for his task. The campaign against Satan begins. "The reason the Son of God appeared was to destroy the works of the devil" (1 John 3:8). This event brings Satan into action. Jesus must not even start. A clever and truly diabolical attempt is made to divert him from his mission.

The tempter fights on three typical fronts. He first attacks the body of Jesus, which a long fast in the desert has weakened. "If you are the Son of God, command these stones to become loaves of bread" (Matt. 4:3). A spiritual temptation comes next. He whom God has commissioned should test his sonship and prove it visibly to others. To give weight to his demand the tempter even quotes Holy Scripture (Matt. 4:6; Ps. 91:11-12). Satan finally goes for the jugular. He promises Jesus power and dominion if he will bow down and worship him. Jesus may either make a pact with the devil and have the guarantee of achieving power, or he may stick to God's commission which can and will lead to weakness. This is the final choice.

The story reminds us in many ways of the account of the temptation of Adam and Eve. There the serpent asked the suggestive question: "Did God say?" Smoothly including a saying of God, he tried successfully to raise doubts about the divine mandate. Satan uses a similar strategy in the encounter with Jesus: "If you are the Son of God, command . . . If you are the Son of God, throw yourself down . . ." Unlike Adam, however, Jesus, the second Adam, remains true to God's promise. Faced with satanic temptation, he relies on the only armament that is of any avail at this point, the Word of God. Three times he answers from the Word, the last time with the basic confession of Israel: "You shall worship the Lord your God, and him only shall you serve" (Matt. 4:10; cf. Deut. 6:13).

It is worth noting that all the things to which Satan alludes, and which he holds out in prospect for Jesus, actually took place on the way of the gospel, but not at all as Satan proposed. Jesus gave bread to the hungry, for example, at the feeding of the five thousand. He plunged into the abyss of suffering, death, and dereliction, and was saved by God. He has all power in heaven and on earth (Matt. 28:18). But he achieved these things, not by the use of power or propaganda, but by service and sacrifice. The essential temptation with which Satan confronted Jesus was finally the temptation to avoid the cross, to try to reach his goal by broader and more pleasant paths. The church and Christians today should still note that the goal of faith, and especially that of credible witness and mission, is not to be reached by worldly means. Krister Stendahl remarks: "Madison Avenue techniques for selling the Gospel. We all know that it works. But we should learn: one does not sell Jesus as one sells toothpaste. There is the cross, there is the mystery. And there is God's time, the right time."[6]

An essential affirmation of apostolic faith is that our temptation story is taken up into that of Jesus. The book of Hebrews especially lays heavy stress on the solidarity of the tempted Jesus with our temptation: "For we have not a high priest who is unable to sympathize with our weaknesses, but one who in every respect has been tempted as we are, yet without sinning" (4:15). Jesus has come into the bundle of human life and expressly entered into vulnerability to temptation, though in the same situation he does not tread our infamous way, the way of the old Adam, but takes his own new path, opening it up for us, the path of the new Adam. He does all this, not for himself alone, but for us, effectively to save us. "For because he himself has suffered and been tempted, he is able to help those who are tempted" (2:18).

This christological dimension has a special place in the New Testament view of temptation. We are not left alone in our fallibility and fall. We stand or fall in the power of the story of his temptation. Even in face of satanic temptation, for which we are no match, we are not exposed without defense or protection. The magic of Satan and his demons is demythologized. The devilish cycle of temptation is broken. At the foot of the cross and in the light of the resurrection we need not lose all hope even when facing the final temptation. It is not that we have a tri-

6. Stendahl, "Your Kingdom Come," *Cross Currents* 32 (1982) 264-65.

umphalist certainty of victory. Self-assurance leads back into the vicious circle. We can triumph on the way of Jesus, beneath the cross. In his power we may pray with sober confidence: "And lead us not into temptation."

Does God Lead into Temptation?

In our deliberations thus far we have come close to an understanding of the sixth petition of the Lord's prayer, but the true interpretative problem is still before us. Our survey of the various layers of the biblical concept of temptation has shown us that in addition to human tempting of God and the manifold tests to which we are subject in everyday life as faith is assaulted and proved, there is also, as seen especially in the temptation of Jesus on our behalf, the final eschatological temptation, the satanic challenge which poses an absolute threat to our human destiny. Although all the strata of the *peirasmos* motif come into the picture in the sixth petition, it can hardly be contested that the Lord's Prayer has this ultimate danger especially in view.

But precisely in this regard the Lord's prayer poses a very acute theological and human problem. It is understandable and justifiable that in this danger we should turn to God. But why use the words "Lead us not into temptation?" Does our God, this God, our Father in heaven, lead into such temptation?

The Roman Catholic theologian Jean Carmignac, whose monograph on the text of the Lord's Prayer is a particularly comprehensive contribution, and who has assembled rich materials precisely on this petition, formulates the decisive question as follows: "'Lead us not into temptation'—this statement astonishes anyone who understands that God is infinitely good and that he 'tempts no one' (Jas. 1:13). For when we beseech God not to lead us into temptation, the only reason to do so is that there might be some danger that he would lead us into temptation. We thus run up against a final and incontestable dilemma. On the one hand, if God plays even the tiniest positive role in temptation to

142

sin, he cannot be infinitely good, for he is helping to draw his earthly children into the greatest misery. On the other hand, if God plays no positive role, then we insult him by asking him not to do evil, just as we would be insulted if someone attributed to us a wicked proposal that we never entertained."[7]

This question does not occupy theological and philological specialists alone but also many thoughtful laypeople. I have had intense discussions with friends for whom this formulation has been an obstacle they could not overcome on the way to a Christian understanding of God. What kind of a God is it that leads into such temptation, or that might do so? For those who set great store by the honesty and integrity of the act of faith, it seems hard to believe in such a God. Clarification is needed.

In the New Testament already one may detect traces of a dialog about a possible understanding or misunderstanding of the statement. I have James in mind. Carmignac alluded to 1:13, and I will give the passage in full: "Let no one say when he is tempted, 'I am tempted by God'; for God cannot be tempted by evil and he himself tempts no one; but each person is tempted when he is lured and enticed by his own desire" (1:13-14). James categorically denies here that God might be the driving force behind temptation. Paul also considers the problem in an attempt at clarification and differentiation: "No temptation has overtaken you that is not common to man. God is faithful, and he will not let you be tempted beyond your strength, but with the temptation will also provide the way of escape, that you may be able to endure it" (1 Cor. 10:13).

From apostolic times onward these passages have encouraged commentators on the Lord's Prayer not to take the sixth petition in its strict sense as a statement about God but to look for modalities of a more concrete (and usually less stringent) understanding. Following Carmignac, I will mention some of these.

Paul offered a first possibility in the verse just quoted. God does not lead into temptation, or at least into temptation that we

---

7. Carmignac, *Recherches sur le "Notre Père,"* pp. 237-38.

cannot endure. He blunts the tempter's power, providing an escape from even the most tangled situation. Along such lines the fathers often use phrases like this: "Lead us not into temptation that we cannot endure" (Ambrose). But this interpretation opens the door to another softening, "Let us not be led" for "Lead us not." For centuries both suggestions have been made. Others have referred to the different meanings of the Greek *peirasmos*, citing other languages that have two terms for the one Greek word (as we have shown already, e.g., *probatio* and *tentatio*). God can lead us into a test with good in view, but not into temptation to evil. As Polanus said, there is a difference between temptation as test and temptation as seduction. Many exegetes have sought another way of softening the harsh sense of the petition by distinguishing between God's active and passive activity (causality) as regards temptation. God does not actively lead into temptation; he leaves those whom he would punish in a situation of temptation. Thus Polanus says: "If God wants to punish someone, he abandons him, withdraws from him his grace . . . and hands him over to Satan that he may thrust him into sins."[8]

From a human standpoint we can understand the basic intention of all such interpretations and theologically we can respect it. These interpreters want to protect God, the Father in heaven, against active participation in the menacing event of temptation. It is right to interpret the saying in the broader context of the story of Jesus and therefore specifically in the light of his liberating view of God. But these well-meaning attempts all suffer from the fact that to a large extent they manipulate the text of the petition, forcing it in the desired direction. Hence we can understand commentators with a stronger exegetical orientation when they find an irreconcilable contradiction in the petition and leave it open in view of the unfathomable mystery of evil. Thus Julius Schniewind stated that we are confronted here by an insoluble contradiction of human thought.[9]

---

8. Polanus, *Syntagma*, IX, XVII, 3970.
9. Schniewind, *Das Evangelium nach Mattäus*, 11th ed. (Göttingen: 1964), p. 88.

We must take seriously the warning against impatient and desperate attempts at premature and one-sided resolution of the tension that is undoubtedly present in the petition. We must respect the mystery of evil. Yet I do not believe that respectful silence can be our last word in efforts at interpretation. If there are no easy answers, we may find certain approximations helpful.

Greater attention to the verb used in the petition might point us to the right path. The verb *eispherein* is a word of time but the New Testament almost always uses it spatially. It means "to cause something or someone to be brought from one place to another." The use may be literal or metaphorical. As regards the present problem, it is important to refer to the Gethsemane story. There Jesus tells his sleepy disciples more than once: "Watch and pray that you may not enter into temptation" (Matt. 26:41; cf. vv. 38, 40, 45). Here again the word, with spatial connotations, means being brought into, or entering, the sphere or spell of temptation. In the hour of supreme temptation we must mobilize all the powers of resistance, especially watchful prayer, thought, and action, so as not to come under the spell of temptation, to become its victims, unprepared and helpless. Origen already had a profound sense of the meaning of the petition when he said that we pray for deliverance from temptation, not that we may not be tempted, which is impossible for us on earth, but that we may not fall victim to temptation. On his view those who fall victim to temptation enter into it, for they are caught in its snares.[10]

At first glance this view seems to be just another way of softening the statement. Yet more recent philological research supports it. Carmignac alludes to the careful work of Johannes Heller in 1901 which argues for it on the basis of a syntactical examination of Semitic negations. On Heller's view the meaning is: "Let us not be caught in the sphere of temptation," that is, "Do not let us correspond or conform to temptation."[11] The correctness of this interpretation finds confirmation in the fact

---

10. Origen, *On Prayer* 29, 9; Migne, XI, 536.
11. Carmignac, *Recherches sur le "Notre Père,"* pp. 279, 292-93.

that the New Testament offers us a clear positive alternative to the sixth petition, namely, entering the kingdom of God (Matt. 19:23) or entering into life (19:17).

We have here the final decision in human life. It is God's final decision regarding us. In Matthew 25:31-46 the righteous enter into life, the accursed into eternal punishment, the last judgment. According to God's judgment, and above all the gospel invitation, it is also our own final decision, our yes or no to the kingdom of God. The invitation of Jesus is unequivocal. The thrust of his saving work is not a no but a clear yes to us, a yes to life. This is our hope and confidence. The kingdom of God comes, the kingdom of temptation goes. But its going is full of dangers. The traps of temptation lurk at every step. "The ancient prince of hell, hath risen with purpose fell; Strong mail of craft and power He weareth in this hour; On earth is not his fellow" (Martin Luther).

This apocalyptic aspect, and with it the relevance of the petition, perhaps make more sense in our age than earlier. It calls for sober distinction. In our human world, characterized by sin, there are temptations that we can overcome both individually and as a race. But there are also processes and trends in which temptation escalates to a point of no return, developments which at first perhaps are harmless or even creative but which unleash destructive forces that against our best intentions lead us steeply down into the power of evil, into snares. There is as it were an undertow of evil. This is true in individual temptations, in our own specific temptations. We have only to think of the addiction to drugs, and of other addictions as well. The same applies to the race as a whole. In modern processes of science and progress, do we not come up against areas in which the creativity we strive for threatens to turn into unimaginable destructivity? In which our creative playing with the fire of knowledge threatens to produce an inextinguishable conflagration? For the future of humanity this is a decisive question. We no longer have a handle on the answer; thinking and rethinking are needed. It is time to watch and pray. The shock treatment of the sixth petition forces us and encourages us to do so: "And lead us not into temptation."

But Deliver Us from Evil

The Last Cry

Rudolph Bohren has pointed out that the Lord's Prayer begins with God's innermost being in the light that no eye can gaze upon: "Hallowed be thy name."[1] Then the center of the prayer concerns human bread. Finally, however, it goes down to the deepest hell and the cry goes up: "Deliver us from evil." The arc of the prayer spans the whole of cosmic reality with its heights and its depths. The sequence of the individual petitions is important in this regard. Luther made this point impressively: "Now note that deliverance from evil is the very last thing that we do and ought to pray for. Under this heading we count strife, famine, war, pestilence, plagues, even hell and purgatory, in short, everything that is painful to body and soul. Though we ask for release from all of this, it should be done in a proper manner and at the very last. Why? There are some, perhaps many, who honor and implore God and his saints solely for the sake of deliverance from evil. They have no other interest and do not ever think of the first petitions which stress God's honor, his

1. Bohren, *Das Unser Vater—heute*, p. 116.

name, and his will. Instead, they seek their own will and completely reverse the order of this prayer."[2]

Luther is right. This is our everyday temptation. We often pray the first petitions of the Lord's Prayer as if they were just liturgical forms. Only later do we wake up existentially, perhaps when praying for bread, but certainly in the last petition about menaces and threats: "Deliver us from evil." It is important to let ourselves be told that the Lord's Prayer is an indivisible whole. We must put ourselves into all seven petitions. We must respect the prayer's priorities, first hallowing God's name, seeking his kingdom, doing his will. But even in so doing we should not overlook the fact that this seventh petition is also part of the whole: "Deliver us from evil."

It is the last petition, the last cry. The word "cry" draws attention to the special urgency of the request. This urgency may be detected in the Greek text and in most modern translations. A word like "deliver" may sound as though it belongs to the traditional vocabulary of religion and thus lose some of the force, but the Greek term, which occurs relatively rarely in the New Testament, has a special vividness and dynamic: *rhyomai*, "to save, to rescue, to extricate."

The term "deliver" has this sense in the Old Testament in many different situations. For example, the psalmist can pray: "Rescue me and deliver me from the many waters, from the hand of aliens" (Ps. 144:7); "Deliver me, O Lord, from my enemies" (143:9; cf. 18:17; 59:1; etc.); "Rescue the weak and the needy; deliver them from the hand of the wicked" (82:4). And deliverance not merely from others but from oneself: "Deliver me from all my transgressions" (39:8), indeed, from all "troubles" (34:17; 54:7). This is typical usage in the Psalter. But we find it elsewhere as well. Ezra speaks of being delivered "from the hand of the enemy and from ambushes on the way" (Ezra 8:31). In 1 Chronicles 16:35 David speaks of deliverance "from among the nations." Jeremiah in 15:21 says in God's name: "I will deliver you out of the hand of the wicked, and redeem you from the grasp of

2. Luther, "Exposition of the Lord's Prayer," p. 78.

the ruthless." The book of Wisdom speaks of deliverance from every trouble (16:8). Job sums it all up in 5:19-20: "He will deliver you from six troubles; in seven there shall no evil touch you. In famine he will redeem you from death, and in war from the power of the sword."

According to the witness of the Old Testament, God's saving faithfulness and power are no less comprehensive than human need. In its sparing use of the term, the New Testament adopts Old Testament usage, mostly in direct allusions and quotations. Romans 11:26 expresses the messianic expectation of Israel as follows: "The Deliverer will come from Zion, he will banish ungodliness from Jacob." Colossians 1:13 says of Christ's redeeming work: "He has delivered us from the dominion of darkness and transferred us to the kingdom of his beloved Son." 1 Thessalonians 1:10 describes Jesus directly as the one "who delivers us from the wrath to come," the basis of our hope, and 2 Timothy 4:18 confesses accordingly: "The Lord will rescue me from every evil and save me for his heavenly kingdom." Perhaps alluding to the seventh petition of the Lord's Prayer, Peter writes that "the Lord knows how to rescue the godly from trial" (2 Pet. 2:9). If the New Testament goes beyond the common basis in its use of *rhyomai,* the new feature is the eschatological awareness that sustains and influences most of the verses quoted. This awareness sharpens the sense of the seriousness of the situation, of the depth of the threat to us. It also strengthens faith in the reality and closeness of the deliverance. This combination—the tension-laden dialetic of the two eschatological motifs, to which we shall return—determines the background and atmosphere of the petition "Deliver us from evil."

The Evil One or Evil

"Deliver us from evil." Let us consider the term "evil" (Greek *poneros*). How are we to understand it? From what are we praying to be delivered? Here arises a classical problem in the history of expounding the Lord's Prayer. Do we have a reference to evil in the general sense or to the evil one in a personified sense, that is, to Satan? This question has no simple answer. Philologically, both neuter and masculine are possible, whether in Greek or in many other languages. Even when we look at the many-faceted biblical usage, the question remains open. One may find different emphases in the different biblical witnesses, and they suggest (though not exclusively) different options.

The general understanding of "evil" seems to prevail in the Old Testament. We have already given many examples in connection with the word "deliver." These depict a whole series of situations that might be described as encounters with the phenomenon of evil. First, there are evil people: enemies, the ungodly, the violent, those who lie in wait, oppressors, and liars. Then there are evil circumstances: bondage, poverty, sickness, natural disasters, human misery in every form. There is also our own evil heart, our propensity and vulnerability to evil. All these things figure in the biblical understanding of humanity and the world. The prayer "Deliver us from evil" relates fundamentally to the total and varied field of evil. In this sense the general use, as in the expression "from all evil," seems to justify the neuter form as appropriate.

In the New Testament, too, we find many instances of *poneros* in a general sense. All the Old Testament situations of temptation and threat are present in the New Testament as well. Evil people (Matt. 22:10; 13:49), evil circumstances (2 Tim. 4:18), evil thoughts (Matt. 15:19)—they are all there in the experience of the world of the Evangelists and apostles. The overpowering might of evil threatening us from within and without is felt and suffered with particular force in the New Testament. I have in mind the shattering analysis of the human condition that Paul gives in Romans 7:13-25, leading to a climax in the cry: "Wretched man that I am! Who will deliver me from this body of death?"

The distinctive feature of New Testament usage, however, is that in it, with the awareness of the eschatologically enhanced

150

power and aggressiveness of evil, the masculine form is common alongside the neuter: the evil one, the supreme enemy, Satan, the devil. We have already come across this sinister figure in expounding the sixth petition: Satan the tempter. Certain passages in the New Testament call Satan "the evil one." According to G. Harder, "This is a distinctive NT usage for which no models have been found in the world into which primitive Christianity came."[3] Thus in Matthew 13:19, in the parable of the sower, Satan is undoubtedly meant by "the evil one" who "comes and snatches away what is sown" in the heart. The same is true in Ephesians 6:16, which speaks of "all the flaming darts of the evil one." The equation of "evil" with the devil is especially common in 1 John, as in 2:13, which praises young Christians "because they have overcome the evil one."

Undoubtedly, then, the masculine is possible in the Bible as well as the neuter. Which are we to choose here? Modern New Testament scholars are divided on the point. Ernst Lohmeyer argues for the masculine in line with his view of temptation in the sixth petition. He opted there for an eschatological and apocalyptic understanding of temptation, and in so doing, since the sixth and seventh petitions are closely related, he set the stage for a similar view of evil. Against an eschatological and apocalyptic background, the sharply personalized figure of the evil one, the absolute challenger of God, fits better. Lohmeyer's arguments, supported at many points exegetically, are very convincing. Yet G. Harder concludes that they are not adequate and that the neuter is to be preferred. He adduces prayers from the New Testament world, for example: "Deliver me from every evil thing." Such prayers request "deliverance from temptation, shame, evil impulse, evil events and sickness, evil thoughts and dreams, and consequently from *poneron* in the sense of the evil and the bad. The ref. here, of course, is to daily rather than ultimate deliverance from these. A further pt. is that *ryesthai apo* or *ek* does not refer to the devil in the NT but to men (R. 15:31; 2 Th. 3:2; 2 Pt. 2:7) and powers (2 C. 1:10 [death]; 2 Tm. 3:11 [persecu-

3. G. Harder, *TDNT*, 6:558.

151

tions]; 2 Tm. 4:17 [the lion's mouth]; 2 Tm. 4:18 [every evil]; 2 Pt. 2:9 [temptations])."[4]

The matter being so ambiguous, it is not surprising that in the history of exposition scholars have taken different paths according to their theological preconceptions. The rule in the early church was that the Greek fathers from Origen to Gregory Nazianzus and Maximus the Confessor referred "evil" to the devil, while the Latins, especially under Augustine's influence, mostly championed the more general neuter sense. The Reformers on the whole followed the Latins. The decision for one or the other possibility is closely linked to a prior fundamental decision in the understanding of salvation.

We recall that the early church worked out two basic types of teaching about redemption. The Greek fathers, especially Irenaeus and the great Cappadocians, adopted the classical soteriological approach which Gustav Aulén has described as Christus Victor soteriology.[5] The work of redemption and reconciliation is Christ's warfare and victory. A dramatically dualistic understanding of the world forms the background to this conception. Our human world, and indeed the whole cosmos, has become enslaved to the powers of corruption, the chief of which is the devil. Through the Fall the devil and his consorts seized power in the cosmos. So long as they rule there is enmity between God and the world. The human race has thus fallen under a twofold slavery to sin and to the superior demonic powers, and also under the threat of God's wrath and judgment.

Into this fatal vicious circle comes Jesus Christ. In him God marches toward us, moving into the real conditions of our enslavement, as is very vividly depicted in the Gospels when Jesus drives out demons. In far-ranging discussions Paul thought this out in terms of the implications of Christ's resurrection for the spheres of the principalities and powers. The way of the Son of God means a life-and-death battle. It cost Christ his own life; he

---

4. Ibid., p. 561.
5. See Gustav Aulén, *Christus Victor*, tr. A. G. Hebert (New York: Macmillan, repr. 1969).

died on the cross. Yet this cross was not a hopeless tragedy. It was the site of a triumph. The fathers described the drama of the cross in pictures that were fresh, vivid, and mythological. The devil, they said, could not hold the sinless Jesus in death. He lost his rights. Christ outwitted him. He did not see that Christ's humanity concealed his deity. He thus failed at the very point where he seemed to have won his final victory, at the cross of Christ. De jure and de facto his kingdom has become a broken, judged, and defeated kingdom. Yet even if only for a limited time, he is still dangerous in a last and truly apocalyptic revolt. We who live in this time need to pray with eschatological urgency, with a sharp and concentrated glance at this devilish danger: "Deliver us from evil."

The Latin fathers fully appreciated the danger. But their concern is not so much with the devil and his forces; it is more with sin and its destructive consequences. The problems at the center of their attention are legal and moral rather than mythical and ontological. Along these lines Anselm in particular offers a developed theory in his doctrine of satisfaction. The negative background of redemption is the reality of the Fall. Anselm has a sharp eye for sin. It is a dishonoring of God. In the Fall we betray our Creator and thereby plunge creation into disorder. How is God to react against this attack on his honor and his creation? Anselm adopts the strict slogan of Tertullian: Either punishment or satisfaction (*aut poena aut satisfactio*). But punishment does not come into the question for God, the faithful Creator. For the penalty of sin is death. In view of the cosmic reach of sinful alienation, this would entail the destruction of creation as a whole. The only way open, then, is that of satisfaction. This is the way of Jesus as he treads the path of sacrifice for many. The cross is the price of sin; it brings to light the depths of evil. Face to face with the Crucified, Anselm can thus cry out that we have not yet considered the true weight of sin. Only here do we see how serious evil is, and how serious is our own guilt in the world of evil.

These two different views of redemption mean two different perspectives in theological wrestling with the mystery of evil. We can well understand why the Greek fathers favored the masculine in the seventh petition, the Latin fathers the neuter. But even more important than the differences is the common basis. In both views the cross of Christ is strikingly at the center. In the light or shadow of it, both see how radical, destructive, and costly evil is. Against the dark background of sin the one detects the figure of the tempter, the other focuses on the many-faceted guilt of the tempted, but these are not really alternatives. From different angles they both have in view the same demonic circle, the mystery of evil, which we cannot fully comprehend from any one angle. Biblically, this is a mystery of unfathomable depth, of the abyss that is indicated by the figure of Satan. It has also a shoreless breadth that is denoted by the concept of sin (original sin). The two lines intersect in the biblical term *poneros*.

So-Called Evil

We now return to the petition "Deliver us from evil." Our excursus into the early church has led us to the conclusion that we do not have to decide for one or other of the two exegetically possible options in the understanding of evil, the masculine or the neuter. Both are worth considering. Both carry notable emphases. We need not choose one and reject the other. We can and should agree with Calvin: "It makes very little difference whether we understand by the word 'evil' the devil or sin. Indeed, Satan himself is the enemy who lies in wait for our life [I Peter 5:8]; moreover, he is armed with sin to destroy us. This, then, is our plea: that we may not be vanquished or overwhelmed by any temptations but may stand fast by the Lord's power against all hostile powers that attack us. This is not to succumb to temptations."[6]

Our task in any case is to attest and communicate the knowledge of the human situation in the world of evil that is

6. Calvin, *Institutes*, 2:914, § 3.20.46.

154

common to both options. This knowledge has two components. One is the biblical view of the radical nature of evil in our human world, and also its omnipresence. But the other is the perspective of eschatological hope on the basis of the cross and resurrection of Jesus Christ. The two elements come together in the petition "Deliver us from evil." And both are relevant. Let us attempt to present both components.

To most contemporaries the biblical stress on the seriousness of the human situation in the world seems to be exaggerated and even distorted. It is true that today, in contrast to the immediate past, there is awareness of the explosiveness of problems. The mass media flood us daily with accounts of destructive events: wars, famines, the oppression of groups and peoples, the poisoning of nature, torture, commercialized power, obscenity. Not merely individual phenomena but the problem of evil as such can claim our attention. Best-sellers in contemporary literature are devoted to "so-called evil." Sociologists, scientists, psychologists, and educators regard the manifold destructive phenomena as a pressing challenge and engage in detailed inquiries into their background and ramifications.

But this focusing on evil has little to do with the biblical view of the problem. It is dominated by tendencies to dissolve the reality of moral evil (not to speak of metaphysical evil) and the experience of guilt either into questions of psychological motivation, into the context of social development, or into models of biological behavior. Evil is thus a partial sickness, not a sickness unto death. Certain spheres of the human constitution and human culture are regarded as marginal according to the anthropological presuppositions of this or that theory. Since other spheres and especially human nature as such are intact, therapeutic measures can cure evil. In principle we have it under control. A point that calls for notice is that modern discussions prefer regularly to speak of "so-called evil."

In contrast, the petition "Deliver us from evil" reminds us that the thing we call evil is really evil. The petition gives it its sinister name: evil or the evil one. It stands opposed to any minimizing or devaluing of the problem. Evil as sin is not an occasional lapse. It is a force that threatens and dominates the whole world. "None is righteous, no, not one; no one understands, no one seeks for God. All have turned aside, together they have gone wrong; no one does good, not even one" (Rom. 3:10-12; cf. Ps. 14:1-3). Nor does sin affect only marginal areas of human life compared to which there are healthy areas and powers. It affects and alienates the very center of life, the heart: "The heart is deceitful above all things, and desperately corrupt" (Jer. 17:9; cf. the saying of Jesus in Matt. 15:19: "For out of the heart come evil thoughts, murder, adultery, fornication, theft, false witness, slander"). This view of ubiquitous and radical evil warns us against illusions and counsels soberness and realism in analyses of the phenomena of evil and encounters with it. We do not finally have it under control.

How do we come to see the relevance of this dark emphasis in the biblical perspective? I would say by way of the bitter experience that obvious illusions about the place of evil lead to tragic disillusionment. Reinhold Niebuhr said all that needs to be said about this in his book *Children of Light and Children of Darkness*. He uses the term "children of light" for the optimistic, humanistic movements of the modern age: liberal, democratic, emancipatory, reformist, socialist. Most of them have formulated progressive ideals and made some progress. But all of them to various degrees suffer from the same illusion. They rest on an optimistic view of human nature. They thus promote shortsighted and for the most part unrealistic expectations that they can effectively and decisively reduce and even overcome human alienation by programs. They are wrong about this, and sooner or later they fail. It is striking how often yesterday's revolutionaries become tomorrow's tyrants, how often young reformers become mature and resigned skeptics. Sober insight into the omnipresence of evil can help us to avoid such depressing changes and open up for us more reliable paths.

We may say two things about this matter from a Christian standpoint. First, we must stress that it is not futile but that we are in fact commanded to fight all manifestations of evil and evil tendencies, to engage in opposition and protest against all relationships in which people become degraded, enslaved, oppressed, contemptible beings.[7] Concretely, we have many things to learn from the "children of light." But the other biblical stress is that we must do all this with the sober, biblically clarified awareness that in this battle, on this side of God's kingdom, we will never reach a stage, whether as individuals or the race, at which evil is behind us as a problem that we have definitely mastered, at which we have solved the problem of evil, at which it is no longer necessary but has become superfluous, along with attempts to check its effects, to pray "Deliver us from evil."

Praying in Hope

We now turn to the second unmistakable element in the petition in either the masculine or the neuter form. This is the element of promise and hope. The petition warns us not only against minimizing evil but also against compromising with it. Paradoxically, this is related to the very deep understanding of evil. If the biblical concept of evil is linked to the motifs of Satan and sin, there is obviously a summons to battle here. We cannot come to terms with Satan or make a deal with him. We can only resist him. "Resist the devil, and he will flee from you" (Jas. 4:7). As regards sin, in the Bible it is not a fate hanging over us or an immutable human condition but a misuse of freedom. We are thus called to responsibility in the world of evil. Biblical seriousness about sin has nothing whatever to do with fatalistic tendencies such as we sometimes find in religion (e.g., in Indian religions or Gnosticism). On the contrary, New Testament faith is a resistance movement against fatalism.

The element of hope and promise comes fully to light when we look at the word "deliver" in the petition. We have seen

7. Cf. the young Karl Marx, *Die Frühschriften*, ed. S. Landshut (Stuttgart: Kröner, 1953), p. 216.

already that the New Testament clearly relates deliverance to the Easter story, especially to the cross. There on the cross the seventh petition was answered.[8] With this petition we do not encounter the experiences and threats of evil as unarmed objects that have no chance against the superior forces opposing us. Nor do we have a handle on evil, as already said. Yet from the standpoint of the Lord's Prayer, evil, though not in our grasp—we must have no illusions on that score—is in the grasp of God— there is no place for disillusionment here. We pray in the power of redemption. Note what W. Pfendsack said. We do not pray (merely) for future victory, redemption, deliverance. We pray on the basis of the victory of Jesus Christ already won. Whatever may still be said about evil, however we experience its power in our world and our lives, and no matter how we may fare personally in the battle with it, after Golgotha there is no longer any evil in this world that the event of redemption has not encompassed and bracketed. We have a hope, a goal. We are going toward deliverance.[9]

Perhaps many of us view such strong statements rather skeptically. They sound like solemn Sunday music. Are they real consolation or false consoling? The saying of Marx that religion is the opiate of the people seems suspiciously apt. In fact, we can hardly argue that promises of this kind may not be misunderstood and misused. Thus we misuse them when we use the consolation of deliverance for the purpose of private consoling. This often happens in church circles. The line here is a fine one. Yet we can see the line in the Bible when the promise is motivation, a spur to the corresponding action. Thus in the New Testament the eschatological indicative of redemption becomes the eschatological imperative, the power of liberation. It was so in the apostolic church. Its committed mission across all frontiers, to the whole world, is the best sign of that. With this faith, this prayer, we cannot let the world be. We cannot ignore its troubles and its joys. It is set, as it is, in the perspective of redemption,

8. See W. Lüthi, *Lord's Prayer*, p. 66.
9. Pfendsack, *Unser Vater*, p. 94.

and it must experience this in the word and deed of Christian witness.

In his exposition of the petition, Lüthi draws out the implications as follows. "He [the Christian] can in fact no longer put up with the wretchedness of this world, with war and famine, disease and earthquakes. He can no longer say that all this is fate and therefore unavoidable. He knows now that in all circumstances of wretchedness in this world there is something we can do: we need not be silent, but can cry out, 'Save us! Free us from it!' Once a man has tasted the salvation of Christ, then he will not easily rid himself of hunger and thirst for the better world that is to come."[10]

Note well, this is the future world of God, not a private paradise for the devout soul. Once again, and for the last time, we turn our attention to the little pronoun in the petition: "Deliver *us* from evil." Not just *me*—though I am certainly included—but *us*. The deliverance for which we pray is not for me alone but for us. The hope is for us, for humanity, indeed, for all creation. Precisely the eschatological, apocalyptic background of the seventh petition—whose allusions to the sinister forces of evil many have wanted to eliminate as mythological—breaks open the protected private zones that we religious folk like to set up around ourselves and cultivate, and broadens our outlook into one of solidarity with all our fellows and indeed with all creatures.

Ebeling has some apt words on this theme.

> If our hearts and minds are awake as we cast ourselves and our fate upon this word, "Deliver us from evil," then we become contemporaries of all who suffer and cry out for deliverance. Then we cannot say, "What are the starving masses in India to me?" Then we become contemporaries even with things that seem to belong to the past, such as the gas chambers of Auschwitz—but how could such a thing ever become a thing of the past? A sea of torment wells up around us. . . . The suffering of my neighbor is also mine. And when I say, "Deliver us from

10. Lüthi, *Lord's Prayer*, p. 67.

evil," then I am speaking in the name of all, in the name of the world.[11]

This is how Paul at least understood it, especially in Romans 8, in which he spoke about our common destiny of suffering and trouble that links God's children to all creation, and also about the common, indivisible hope, the hope of redemption. It is in this hope that we pray in solidarity with a world that is characterized by mounting threats and afflictions, making our request, "Deliver us from evil," vicariously.

I am convinced that this emphasis in the seventh petition has special relevance today. I was working on the first draft of this exposition in the spring of 1984. How much has been written about Orwell and that year! The negative utopia seems to fit in uncannily well with our present-day fears and anxieties. I have in mind the experiences of the last few weeks. Behind me lies participation in a university forum on anxiety and aggression. Ahead I am invited to join a symposium on false forms of anxiety. On the weekend, when I was working on the text, the *Basler Zeitung* ran a special section that devoted eight pages to a dramatic discussion and depiction of apocalyptic: "Everything Going Down to Destruction?" Since then the crisis and the corresponding mood have hardly lightened. Instead, they have grown darker with Chernobyl and the disaster at the gates of Basel. The apocalypse is at hand.

One might regard the dazzling attractiveness of such apocalyptic inquiries as merely the latest manifestation of a transitory spirit of the age. After the collapse of the positive utopias of the sixties the negative now have their turn. But there is more to it than that. Unfortunately, apocalyptic themes correspond to apocalyptic developments in the world today. We have only to think of the enhanced threat of accumulated arsenals, of famines in large parts of the world, of the death of forests to promote our welfare. With good and terrifying reason we may conclude that the apocalypse is an imminent reality.

11. Ebeling, *On Prayer*, pp. 95-96.

Yet we must distinguish this apocalypse from another. There is the apocalypse that does harm—Cassandra cries that conjure up evil, dark pictures that plunge us into despair and resignation. Theology and the church, however, have occasion and commission to remind people of that other, the biblical, apocalypse. This is somber enough. It knows the depth and power of evil. It bewails and accuses, yet it does not discourage. It does not transfix us with terror. On the contrary, it shakes us up, awakes us, makes us alert. The words and acts of the apostles point in this direction. They enjoin us, as Paul did the Romans: "It is full time now for you to wake from sleep. For salvation is nearer to us now than when we first believed; the night is far gone, the day is at hand. Let us then cast off the works of darkness and put on the armor of light" (Rom. 13:11-12).

Clearly, for the apostle his own world and time had an eschatological and apocalyptic background. But the apocalyptic was that of hope, not of hopelessness. The night is deep but it is passing. It is good for us to look ahead to the morning, to light little lights, and, as Luther said, to plant an apple tree. Is not this the attitude that we and our contemporaries need? The early church read that passage from Romans on the First Sunday of Advent, at the beginning of the Christian year. This was profoundly right. Its sober but confident message must characterize the church's ministry from beginning to end. Even in apocalyptic days, concerned and anxious but not despairing, looking forward to the coming redemption, we thus pray: "Deliver us from evil."

For Thine Is the Kingdom and the Power and the Glory. Amen

Redemption from Ambivalence

An old and much debated question is whether the concluding doxology is the authentic ending of the Lord's Prayer. Historico-critical research now inclines fairly unanimously to the view that we have here an ancient and laudable addition to the original text of the Gospel. The oldest manuscripts do not have it. It is commonly attested only in the Antiochene group and then the Byzantine. Of the fathers, John Chrysostom and Theodore of Mopsuestia consider it, but the Latin fathers, with the Vulgate, do not know it. The Reformers argued (correctly, according to the textual criticism of their time) for its authenticity. For generations a distinguishing mark between Roman Catholics and Protestants was whether they used the doxology.

If the authenticity of the doxology is doubtful from the standpoint of textual criticism, most theologians today, including Roman Catholics, recognize clearly its theological significance. This is not just because doxologies were customary at the end of contemporary Jewish prayers, nor because the Didache includes the doxology in the text of the Lord's prayer, but above all because the words breathe an unequivocally biblical spirit.

Repeatedly and rightly reference has been made to the doxology in one of the great Old Testament prayers, 1 Chronicles 29:11, where David prays: "Thine, O Lord, is the greatness, and the glory, and the victory, and the majesty; thine is the kingdom, O Lord, and thou art exalted as head above all." The New Testament model of prayer, like the Old Testament model, has first and last this plain orientation. Both of them confess and extol the kingdom, the power, and the glory of the Lord.

I believe that in this ending we have more than pious liturgical usage. Here once again and finally our need before God, specifically our need of prayer, is addressed and highlighted in hope. All of us know our weakness in prayer. We drew attention to this at the very beginning of our exposition. Most of us in our secularized lives make heavy going when it comes to prayer. We lack confidence. We are torn by doubts. Often we are only halfhearted.

But then we find an illuminating saying in James in which he exhorts us to pray with confidence and without doubting, "for he who doubts is like a wave of the sea that is driven and tossed by the wind. . . . a double-minded man [is] unstable in all his ways" (Jas. 1:6-8). Who of us can deny that we see ourselves and our prayer life, our need of prayer, in this picture. We are double-minded people. Yet James links to the depiction a disconcerting warning: "That person must not suppose that [he] . . . will receive anything from the Lord." This makes us think. It raises the question whether our prayers reach their mark. Are they futile because of our incontestable weakness? Is the Lord's Prayer futile when we repeat it after Jesus, precisely in face of the dangers that plainly confront us, and especially in the two concluding petitions?

It would be wrong to pay no heed to this warning. We must take it seriously. We must fight this notorious state of double-mindedness, and above all the playing with doubt that especially afflicts theologians. But precisely where we let ourselves be told this, refusing to be reconciled to our weakness in prayer as though it were only a minor theological offense, we must also let ourselves be told the doxology. Thanks be to God, the final hope of our prayer does not rest on us, on the impeccable state of our pious consciousness, important though that may be, but on God's own faithfulness. The little word "for"—coming after the petitions—"And lead us not into temptation, But deliver us from evil"—stands clearly in counterpoint. It represents a Nevertheless to the concentrated power of temptation and evil. Then the "Amen" confesses the assurance that God's faithfulness truly and certainly makes this counterthrust (motifs that are unmistakable in the Hebrew word). For those who pray the Lord's Prayer can hope that they will not be put to shame even and precisely in the ultimate dangers of life that the last two petitions envision.

Putting this idea in a powerful triple form at the end, if I am not mistaken, is the theological and pastoral point of the doxology. The Reformers stated this view with liberating and encouraging force. Luther said that this is our foundation. The gospel commands us not to look at our own good deeds or perfection but at the God of promise himself, at the Mediator Christ himself. This is how our theology achieves its assurance. We are torn away from ourselves and put outside ourselves, so as not to rely on our own powers, conscience, experience, person, or works, but on that which is outside us, namely, on the promise and truth of God which can never deceive us.[1]

We find the same stress in Calvin when he has the following persuasive comments on the ending of the Lord's Prayer: "This is firm and tranquil repose for our faith. For if our prayers were to be commended to God by our worth, who would dare even mutter in his presence? Now, however miserable we may be, though unworthiest of all, however devoid of all commendation, we will yet never lack a reason to pray, never be shorn of assurance, since his Kingdom, power, and glory can never be snatched away from our Father."[2]

In this sense the doxology, for those who pray uncertainly, is a liberating and encouraging affirmation, the expression of a

---

1. *D. Martin Luthers Werke: Kritische Gesamtausgabe,* 40/1:585.
2. Calvin, *Institutes,* 2:915-16, § 3.20.47.

Nevertheless hope. It redeems us from ambivalence and promises and grants to our praying of the Lord's Prayer an impregnable foundation and indestructible goal.

Again the Kingdom

Let us now look separately at the three motifs in the final acclamation. The first, the kingdom, we may deal with briefly. This is not because it is less important than the other two. On the contrary, the kingdom is the central theme of the prayer. It is the only key word that occurs twice. The Lord's Prayer has rightly been called time and again the kingdom prayer.

The very fact that the term occurs twice, however, allows us to refer to our exposition of the petition "Thy kingdom come." We may presuppose this earlier discussion, though with the reminder that we there discerned two different lines, the spatial, concrete, everyday line on the one side, that of God's royal dominion on the other. In the doxology we are to think especially of the second line. It thus corresponds to the doxological tradition of the Old Testament (we recall the parallel in 1 Chron. 29:11) and also in the early church. This is the specific emphasis of the doxology. It is a redemptive reference to the ultimate reality of God which transcends all temptations, principalities, and powers. To whom the final word belongs in our ambivalent world and among us ambivalent people is not in any sense unclear. Jesus Christ is Lord. He is the kingdom in person: *autobasileia tou theou*. To him the future belongs: "For thine is the kingdom."

The concrete implications of this come out in the two words that follow with their own specific accents. We must now look at them in detail.

And the Power

This second term brings us into a specific field of tension in human history, the question of power. Looking ahead to our century, Friedrich Nietzsche once predicted that the future would be controlled by an enhanced will for power and superpower. Our century does in fact stand under the sign of an incomparably enhanced and threatening will for power. This will exploded in the most dreadful wars in human history. It has established an extremely fragile balance of terror; weapons are of a destructive force that is capable of putting an end to life on our planet. Politically, it has found especially solid crystallization in the cynical power systems of Fascism and Stalinism. But as the arrogance of power it is a temptation to other forms of government as well. Economically, it expressed itself in the structures of national and international exploitation, often racist, the victims of which were economically disadvantaged classes and nations. Technological power, which the last century lauded as the engine of progress, soon showed its other face in our day in the form of its potential for technocratic alienation and ecological endangerment.

When the doxology of the Lord's Prayer speaks of the power of God, it posits resistance to all such things. For when the Bible asks concerning God's power, it is soon evident that God has not joined the club of power (C. S. Song). If God's power was manifested on the way of Jesus of Nazareth, if God's word of power became incarnate in him, then the thrust of God's power is not toward graceless superpower, toward compulsion and manipulation, toward ensuring lordship over others, but toward redeeming, winning, and establishing. "For the Son of man also came not to be served but to serve, and to give his life as a ransom for many" (Mark 10:45).

Has this kind of power any chance in the world of graceless powers? Many theologians are not sure. The catchphrase "the impotent God" has replaced "the Almighty" in many circles in modern theology. As a prophetic emphasis this was justifiable, especially in such pioneering thinkers as Dietrich Bonhoeffer or the Czech philosopher Emanuel Rádl who confessed a revolution in the concept of power effected in the history of Jesus. But this important insight becomes a theological trap when only this aspect is heeded, when the triumph of graceless powers fascinates or depresses us, and when God seems to be so powerless in comparison that we no longer dare to speak of his power. This is to ideologize and pervert an important biblical insight.

For the way of Jesus of Nazareth has its other side as well. Inseparably related to the cross is the resurrection. In the experience of the disciples the impotence of Jesus demonstrated the power of God and proved it to be ultimate power, power over the last enemy, over death. God's power lost in order to win. It won even as it lost. According to the New Testament witness, this power is true power. Concerning it the apostle speaks of "the power of an indestructible life" (Heb. 7:16). Note this expression. Obviously, there are destructible powers of destructible life. We experience them and suffer from them every day. But the gospel tells us that these powers have no lasting validity. They are destructible. Despite appearances to the contrary, they lost their rights in the sacrifice of Christ. Hence they have essentially lost their power before God. They have no future. They are self-destructive. Many claims to power and excesses of power have in fact been wretchedly broken before our very eyes. It is love that truly endures before God and among us. This is the power of an indestructible life, for it never fails (as Paul bears witness in 1 Cor. 13:8). If there really is and can be a new beginning for our power-obsessed world, it will come from forgiving and reconciling love, from the Spirit of grace.

But we must take note of a misunderstanding and possible misuse. Religious orientation to love and grace is exposed to the danger and suspicion of a weak sentimentality. Striving for the heavenly heights of a holy mind and pure ideals, we might neglect the depths of earthly, material relations. Love in the New Testament sense is very different. It is oriented to incarnation, to concrete needs of body, soul, and spirit. Ecumenical social ethics has rightly begun to speak of love through structures and encourages us to take successive initiatives in structural measures that soberly strive for less injustice and more justice.

The Indian ecumenist and economist S. L. Parmar has stated this idea as follows. Structures of injustice are immune to sentimental appeals. Love can be strong only by promoting justice. Opposing injustice is the first step in developing this kind of strength. The prophetic exhortation to "let justice roll down like waters" and the teaching of Jesus that we should love our neighbors as ourselves are integral parts of the force that is needed. Such calls are challenges to the injustice embedded in relations, institutions, and words.

We must try to take two related steps in the light of the doxology "Thine is the power." The first is the step from might to right, the second the step from right to love. Might without right is unlimited, destructive, self-destructive. Right without love threatens to ossify, to become compassionless, to lack grace. Against this background the love that presses on to a higher righteousness (in the sense of the Sermon on the Mount and the Lord's Prayer) serves the interests of right and offers a strategy for the politically necessary restraining of power.

And the Glory

The doxology ends with this third clause, which gives it its name: "doxology." *Doxa* is the Greek word for "glory." The content and significance of the term are unmistakable. But does it not breathe a spirit of triumphalism which seems to be at odds with the spirit and credibility of the gospel?

We must weigh such questions very carefully. A theology of glory, a one-sided emphasizing of the glorious aspect of the Christian life (as opposed to the theology of the cross), would be a dubious enterprise for both theology and the church. Yet this is not the meaning of the doxology "Thine is the glory," nor of "glory" in the Bible as a whole. It is worth noting that the New Testament emphatically understands the glory of God in relation to the history of Jesus, and that in this connection the cross (as well as the resurrection) is of key significance. The glory of God is seen as the glory of the Crucified, the glory of self-sacrificing love.

The Christian community is set in the same light. It shares the glory of its Lord in both his cross and his resurrection. The people of glory are not a glorious people. They do not lead a tension-free, triumphalist life in the perspective of God's glory. Paul expresses this point with particular clarity in 2 Corinthians 4, a passage which bears powerful witness to the glory of God in the lives of Christians. "But we have this treasure in earthen vessels. . . . We are afflicted in every way but not crushed; perplexed, but not driven to despair; persecuted, but not forsaken; struck down, but not destroyed; always carrying in the body the death of Jesus, so that the life of Jesus may also be manifested in our bodies" (vv. 7-10).

The Christian life is seen here in highly dramatic terms. But this drama is not a tragedy. The ambivalence and brokenness of the Christian life do not entail a situation of permanent equipoise. The cross and the resurrection are not equally balanced. "Thine is the kingdom and the power and the glory"; our lives are moving toward this ultimate promise. Thus the same Paul who knows so well the afflictions of the community, and his own, can still dare, in spite of everything, to describe a movement "from glory to glory" (2 Cor. 3:18).

This venture has only one basis, which the apostle also names, that is, the presence of the Spirit. Our confidence can never be that we will finally "make it." The weight of glory that far surpasses our light affliction (2 Cor. 4:17) does not come from our own resources but from the actuality of the Holy Spirit, the power of God. "The Spirit helps us in our weakness" (Rom. 8:26).

The Spirit sets us in motion, seeking to demonstrate his power. Glory calls for glorifying. It is a doxological initiative. Glorifying embraces all life's spheres, both personal and social. It shows itself in many ways in both word and deed. We need think only of the way in which emphasis on the glory of God in

Reformed theology led to democratic political initiatives that were critical of government inasmuch as no political authority can claim ultimate honor or glory.

In what follows I want to stress a dimension of glorifying that has not been given its due in church history, especially in Reformed churches. I refer to the doxological dimension in the narrower sense. One could also speak of the aesthetic dimension of glorifying in terms that might seem strange and suspicious to pious and particularly to Reformed ears. To minimize possible misunderstanding, I will also stress that I am not offering the floor to any theological aestheticism. The glory of God is not a show that one can watch as one does a television show. Nevertheless, we miss a vital aspect if we ignore the fact that the most obvious response to *doxa* is a doxological attitude. Primarily, this word means praise, adoring prayer to God. This response has no utilitarian or calculable goal. It is a liturgy of freedom, a celebration of joy.

Such an attitude contains the aesthetic dimension of glorifying. Some of the classical (Reformed) catechisms describe it as our chief end to glorify God and to enjoy him for ever. An element of delight, desire, and enjoyment is part of the response to God's glory. I agree with Jürgen Moltmann's remark about the Lord of glory: that as exalted, transfigured, and changed man he works on us lowly and inhuman mortals, not merely by liberating power and new demands, but by his perfection and beauty. These aesthetic categories of the resurrection, he says, are part of the new life in faith. Without them the discipleship of Christ and the new obedience would be joyless, legal labor.[3]

Attempts to live in the light of the Lord's Prayer must not leave out this dimension of the beautiful and this atmosphere of joy, especially in view of the straining and compulsion to achieve which govern and pervert so much in our lives, even in the church. There is nothing to be said against work. But there is everything to be said against works-righteousness, against the attempt to justify ourselves and our systems. The struggle for

3. Moltmann, *Kirche in der Kraft des Geistes* (Munich: Kaiser, 1975), p. 128.

self-righteousness and works-righteousness, the urge to vindi-
cate—perhaps that is the great temptation of our day.

In obscuring God's glory and losing transcendence, we
only too easily become the prisoners of immanence and the
slaves of self-made, asthmatic anxiety. But Jesus, the witness to
the glory of God, leads us out of the grip of such anxiety, opens
our eyes to the future of the kingdom of God, and in this liberating light opens them also to the beauties of creation: "Consider
the lilies of the field, how they grow; they neither toil nor spin;
yet I tell you, even Solomon in all his glory was not arrayed like
one of these" (Matt. 6:28-29). In this way the distorted standards
of humanity are corrected and the true priorities are set: "Seek
first his kingdom and his righteousness, and all these things
shall be yours as well" (v. 33).

Thus the kingdom of God—and his power and his glory—
becomes the offer of liberating grace and the attack of Jesus on
the alienated gracelessness of human hearts and conditions. In
consequence it becomes the source of joy within creation. The
Lord's Prayer and the doxology encourage us not to dry up this
source but to engage in constant praise of God and advocacy of
his grace in defiance of all the evil spirits of our age.

Bibliography

Barth, Karl. *The Christian Life. Church Dogmatics.* Vol. IV/4: *Lecture Fragments.* Tr. Geoffrey W. Bromiley. Grand Rapids: Eerdmans, 1981.
————. *Prayer According to the Catechisms of the Reformation.* Tr. Sara F. Terrien. Philadelphia: Westminster, 1952.
Die Bekenntnisschriften der Evangelisch-Lutherischen Kirche. 3rd ed. Göttingen: Vandenhoeck & Ruprecht, 1956.
Bekenntnisschriften und Kirchenordnungen der nach Gottes Wort reformierten Kirche. Ed. W. Niesel. Zurich: 1939.
Blumhardt, Johann Christoph. *Das Vaterunser.* 4th ed. Basel: 1946.
Bohren, Rudolf. *Das Unser Vater—heute.* Zurich: 1960.
Bonhoeffer, Dietrich. *Gesammelte Schriften.* Vol. 3. Munich: Kaiser, 1960.
————. *Letters and Papers from Prison: The Enlarged Edition.* Tr. Reginald Fuller, et al. Ed. Eberhard Bethge. New York: Macmillan, 1972.
Calvin, John. *Institutes of the Christian Religion.* 2 vols. Tr. Ford Lewis Battles. Ed. John T. McNeill. Philadelphia: Westminster, 1960.
Carmignac, J. *Recherches sur le "Notre Père."* Paris: Letouzey, 1969.
Ebeling, Gerhard. *On Prayer: The Lord's Prayer in Today's World.* Tr. James W. Leitch. Philadelphia: Fortress, repr. 1978.
Jeremias, Joachim. *The Prayers of Jesus.* Studies in Biblical Theology 2/6. Tr. John Bowden, et al. Naperville, IL: Allenson, 1967.
Köberle, Adolf. *Das Vaterunser und der Mensch in der Gegenwart.* Stuttgart: 1940.
Lochman, Jan Milič. *The Faith We Confess: An Ecumenical Dogmatics.* Tr. David Lewis. Philadelphia: Fortress, 1984.
————. *Im Namen Gottes des Allmächtigen.* Basel: 1982.

————. *Das radikale Erbe, Versuche theologischer Orientierung in Ost und West.* Zurich: 1972.

————. *Reich, Kraft und Herrlichkeit.* Munich: 1981.

————. *Reconciliation and Liberation: Challenging a One-Dimensional View of Salvation.* Tr. David Lewis. Philadelphia: Fortress, 1980.

————. *Signposts to Freedom: The Ten Commandments and Christian Ethics.* Tr. David Lewis. Minneapolis: Augsburg, 1982.

————. *Trägt oder trügt die christliche Hoffnung?* Zurich: 1974.

Lochman, Jan Milič, F. Buri, and H. Ott. *Dogmatik im Dialog.* Vol. 1: *Die Kirche und die Letzten Dinge.* Gütersloh: 1973. Vol. 2: *Theologie, Offenbarung, Gotteserkenntnis.* Gütersloh: 1974. Vol. 3: *Schöpfung und Erlösung.* Gütersloh: 1976.

Lohmeyer, Ernst. *"Our Father": An Introduction to the Lord's Prayer.* Tr. John Bowden. New York: Harper & Row, 1965.

Luther, Martin. "An Exposition of the Lord's Prayer for Simple Laymen, 1519." In *Luther's Works.* Vol. 42: *Devotional Writings.* Ed. Martin O. Dietrich. Tr. Martin H. Bertram. Philadelphia: Fortress, 1969.

Lüthi, Walter. *The Lord's Prayer: An Exposition.* Tr. Kurt Schoenenberger. Richmond, VA: John Knox, 1961.

Nitschke, Horst, ed. *Das Vaterunser.* Gütersloh: 1987.

Pfendsack, Werner. *Unser Vater.* Basel: 1961.

Ragaz, Leonhard. "Das Unservater." In *Von der Revolution der Bibel.* Vol. I. Zurich: 1943.

Stendahl, Krister. "Your Kingdom Come." *Cross Currents* 32/3 (Fall 1982): 257-66.

Index of Scripture References

Index of Names